Simple 1-2-3™

EAGLE BRAND®

Publications International, Ltd.

Favorite Brand Name Recipes at www.fbnr.com

Front cover photography and photography on pages 5, 8, 9, 10, 12, 15, 17, 20, 29, 37, 43, 67, 68, 69, 79, 92, 93, 94, 102, 104, 111, 123, 125, 126, 130, 133, 142, 143, 149 and 154 by Chris Cassidy Photography, Inc.
Photographer: Chris Cassidy
Photographer's Assistant: Gary Joachim
Prop Stylist: Nancy Cassidy
Food Stylists: Carol Smoler, Joanne Witherell
Assistant Food Stylist: Elaine Funk

Pictured on the front cover: Black & White Cheesecake *(page 45)*.

Pictured on the back cover *(left to right):* Choco-Peanut Butter-Brickle Cookies *(page 4)*, Creamy Baked Cheesecake *(page 47)* and Peanut Butter Blocks *(page 149)*.

ISBN-13: 978-1-4127-2347-3
ISBN-10: 1-4127-2347-7

Library of Congress Control Number: 2005910367

Manufactured in China.

8 7 6 5 4 3 2 1

Microwave Cooking: Microwave ovens vary in wattage. Use the cooking times as guidelines and check for doneness before adding more time.

Preparation/Cooking Times: Preparation times are based on the approximate amount of time required to assemble the recipe before cooking, baking, chilling or serving. These times include preparation steps such as measuring, chopping and mixing. The fact that some preparations and cooking can be done simultaneously is taken into account. Preparation of optional ingredients and serving suggestions is not included.

Contents

Cookies

Choco-Peanut Butter-Brickle Cookies

1 (14-ounce) can EAGLE BRAND® Sweetened Condensed Milk (NOT evaporated milk)
1 cup crunchy peanut butter
2 eggs
1 teaspoon vanilla extract
1½ cups all-purpose flour
1 teaspoon baking soda
½ teaspoon baking powder
½ teaspoon salt
1 cup (6 ounces) semisweet chocolate chips
1 cup chocolate-covered toffee bits or almond brickle chips

1. Preheat oven to 350°F. In large bowl, beat EAGLE BRAND®, peanut butter, eggs and vanilla until well blended.

2. In medium bowl, combine flour, baking soda, baking powder and salt. Add to peanut butter mixture; beat until blended. Stir in chocolate chips and toffee bits. Drop by heaping tablespoonfuls onto lightly greased baking sheets.

3. Bake 12 minutes or until lightly browned. Cool slightly on baking sheets; remove to wire racks to cool.   *Makes 3 dozen cookies*

Prep Time: *15 minutes*
Bake Time: *12 minutes*

3½ cups all-purpose flour
2 teaspoons baking powder
¼ teaspoon salt
1 (14-ounce) can EAGLE BRAND® Sweetened Condensed Milk (NOT evaporated milk)
¾ cup (1½ sticks) butter or margarine, softened
2 eggs
1 tablespoon vanilla extract
Colored sugar sprinkles (optional)
Powdered Sugar Glaze (recipe follows, optional)

Cut-Out Cookies

1. Combine flour, baking powder and salt. In large bowl with mixer on low speed, beat EAGLE BRAND®, butter, eggs and vanilla until just blended. Beat on medium speed 1 minute or until smooth. Add flour mixture; beat on low speed until blended. (If using hand-held mixer, use wooden spoon to add last portion of flour mixture.) Divide dough into thirds. Wrap and chill dough 2 hours or until easy to handle.

2. Preheat oven to 350°F. On lightly floured surface, roll out one portion of dough to ⅛-inch thickness. Cut out shapes. Gather dough and re-roll to use entire portion of dough. Repeat with remaining dough portions. Place cut-outs 1 inch apart on ungreased baking sheets. Sprinkle with colored sugar (optional). Bake 9 to 11 minutes or until lightly browned around edges (do not overbake). Cool 5 minutes. Remove cookies to wire racks. When cool, glaze and decorate as desired. Store covered at room temperature.

Makes 5½ dozen cookies

Powdered Sugar Glaze

2 cups sifted powdered sugar
½ teaspoon vanilla extract
2 tablespoons milk or whipping cream
Food coloring (optional)

Whisk powdered sugar and vanilla, adding just enough milk or cream to bind into a glaze consistency. Add food coloring (optional) to tint glaze.

Chocolate Peanut Butter Chip Cookies

1. Preheat oven to 350°F. In large saucepan over low heat, melt chocolate and butter with EAGLE BRAND®; remove from heat. Add biscuit mix, egg and vanilla; with mixer, beat until smooth and well blended.

2. Let mixture cool to room temperature. Stir in peanut butter chips. Shape into 1¼-inch balls. Place 2 inches apart on ungreased baking sheets. Bake 6 to 8 minutes or until tops are lightly crusty. Cool. Store tightly covered at room temperature.

Makes about 4 dozen cookies

Prep Time: *15 minutes*
Bake Time: *6 to 8 minutes*

8 (1-ounce) squares semisweet chocolate
3 tablespoons butter or margarine
1 (14-ounce) can EAGLE BRAND® Sweetened Condensed Milk (NOT evaporated milk)
2 cups biscuit baking mix
1 egg
1 teaspoon vanilla extract
1 cup (6 ounces) peanut butter-flavored chips

Cookies

Double Chocolate Cherry Cookies

1¼ cups (2½ sticks) butter or margarine, softened
1¾ cups sugar
2 eggs
1 tablespoon vanilla extract
3½ cups all-purpose flour
¾ cup unsweetened cocoa
½ teaspoon baking powder
½ teaspoon baking soda
¼ teaspoon salt
2 (6-ounce) jars maraschino cherries, well drained and halved
1 (6-ounce) package semisweet chocolate chips
1 (14-ounce) can EAGLE BRAND® Sweetened Condensed Milk (NOT evaporated milk)

1. Preheat oven to 350°F. In large bowl, beat butter and sugar until fluffy. Add eggs and vanilla; mix well.

2. In large bowl, combine dry ingredients; stir into butter mixture (dough will be stiff). Shape into 1-inch balls. Place 1 inch apart on ungreased baking sheets.

3. Press cherry half into center of each cookie. Bake 8 to 10 minutes. Cool.

4. In heavy saucepan over medium heat, melt chips with EAGLE BRAND®; cook until mixture thickens, about 3 minutes. Frost each cookie, covering cherry. Store loosely covered at room temperature.

Makes about 10 dozen cookies

Prep Time: *25 minutes*
Bake Time: *8 to 10 minutes*

Double Chocolate Pecan Cookies: Prepare and shape dough as directed above, omitting cherries. Flatten. Bake and frost as directed. Garnish each cookie with pecan half.

Chocolate Chip Treasure Cookies

1. Preheat oven to 375°F. In small bowl, combine graham cracker crumbs, flour and baking powder.

2. In large bowl, beat EAGLE BRAND® and butter until smooth. Add crumb mixture; mix well. Stir in coconut, chocolate chips and walnuts.

3. Drop by rounded tablespoonfuls onto ungreased baking sheets. Bake 9 to 10 minutes or until lightly browned. Cool. Store loosely covered at room temperature. *Makes about 3 dozen cookies*

Prep Time: *15 minutes*
Bake Time: *9 to 10 minutes*

1½ cups graham cracker crumbs
½ cup all-purpose flour
2 teaspoons baking powder
1 (14-ounce) can EAGLE BRAND® Sweetened Condensed Milk (NOT evaporated milk)
½ cup (1 stick) butter or margarine, softened
1⅓ cups flaked coconut
1 (12-ounce) package semisweet chocolate chips
1 cup chopped walnuts

Coconut Macaroons

1 (14-ounce) can EAGLE BRAND® Sweetened Condensed Milk (NOT evaporated milk)
1 egg white
2 teaspoons vanilla extract
1 to 1½ teaspoons almond extract
2 (7-ounce) packages flaked coconut (5⅓ cups)

1. Preheat oven to 325°F. Line baking sheets with foil; grease and flour foil. Set aside.

2. In large bowl, combine EAGLE BRAND®, egg white, vanilla and almond extract. Stir in coconut. Drop by rounded teaspoonfuls onto prepared baking sheets; with spoon, slightly flatten each mound.

3. Bake 15 to 17 minutes or until golden. Remove from baking sheets; cool on wire racks. Store loosely covered at room temperature.

Makes about 4 dozen cookies

Prep Time: *10 minutes*
Bake Time: *15 to 17 minutes*

Cookies

Cinnamon Chip Gems

1. In large bowl, beat butter and cream cheese until well blended. Stir in flour, sugar and almonds. Cover; refrigerate about 1 hour. Divide dough into 4 equal parts. Shape each part into 12 smooth balls. Place each ball in small ungreased muffin cup (1¾ inches in diameter); press evenly on bottom and up side of each cup.

2. Preheat oven to 375°F. In small bowl, beat eggs. Add EAGLE BRAND® and vanilla; mix well. Place 7 cinnamon baking chips in bottom of each muffin cup; generously fill three-fourths full with EAGLE BRAND® mixture.

3. Bake 18 to 20 minutes or until tops are puffed and just beginning to turn golden brown. Cool 3 minutes. Sprinkle about 15 chips on top of filling. Cool completely in pan on wire rack. Remove from pan using small metal spatula or sharp knife. Cool completely. Store tightly covered at room temperature.

Makes 4 dozen cookies

Tip: For a pretty presentation, line the muffin pan with colorful paper baking cups before pressing the dough into the muffin cups.

1 cup (2 sticks) butter or margarine, softened
2 (3-ounce) packages cream cheese, softened
2 cups all-purpose flour
½ cup sugar
⅓ cup ground toasted almonds
2 eggs
1 (14-ounce) can EAGLE BRAND® Sweetened Condensed Milk (NOT evaporated milk)
1 teaspoon vanilla extract
1⅓ cups cinnamon baking chips, divided

Easy Peanut Butter Cookies

1 (14-ounce) can EAGLE BRAND® Sweetened Condensed Milk (NOT evaporated milk)
¾ to 1 cup peanut butter
1 egg
1 teaspoon vanilla extract
2 cups biscuit baking mix
Granulated sugar

1. In large bowl, beat EAGLE BRAND®, peanut butter, egg and vanilla until smooth. Add biscuit mix; mix well. Chill at least 1 hour.

2. Preheat oven to 350°F. Shape dough into 1-inch balls. Roll in sugar. Place 2 inches apart on ungreased baking sheets. Flatten with fork in criss-cross pattern.

3. Bake 6 to 8 minutes or until lightly browned (do not overbake). Cool. Store tightly covered at room temperature.   *Makes about 5 dozen cookies*

Prep Time: *10 minutes*
Chill Time: *1 hour*
Bake Time: *6 to 8 minutes*

Peanut Butter & Jelly Gems: Make dough as directed above. Shape into 1-inch balls and roll in sugar; do not flatten. Press thumb in center of each ball of dough; fill with jelly, jam or preserves. Proceed as directed above.

Any-Way-You-Like 'em Cookies: Stir 1 cup semisweet chocolate chips, chopped peanuts, raisins or flaked coconut into dough. Proceed as directed above.

Cookies

Macaroon Kisses

1. Preheat oven to 325°F. Line baking sheets with foil; grease and flour foil. Set aside.

2. In large bowl, combine EAGLE BRAND®, vanilla and almond extract. Stir in coconut. Drop by rounded teaspoonfuls onto prepared baking sheets; with spoon, slightly flatten each mound.

3. Bake 15 to 17 minutes or until golden brown. Remove from oven. Immediately press candy kiss, star or drop in center of each macaroon. Remove from baking sheets; cool on wire racks. Store loosely covered at room temperature.   *Makes 4 dozen cookies*

1 (14-ounce) can EAGLE BRAND® Sweetened Condensed Milk (NOT evaporated milk)
2 teaspoons vanilla extract
1 to 1½ teaspoons almond extract
2 (7-ounce) packages flaked coconut (5⅓ cups)
48 solid milk chocolate candy kisses, stars or drops, unwrapped

Double Chocolate Cookies

2 cups biscuit baking mix
1 (14-ounce) can EAGLE BRAND® Sweetened Condensed Milk (NOT evaporated milk)
8 (1-ounce) squares semisweet chocolate, melted *or* 1 (12-ounce) package semisweet chocolate chips, melted
3 tablespoons butter or margarine, melted
1 egg
1 teaspoon vanilla extract
6 (1¼-ounce) white chocolate candy bars with almonds, broken into small pieces
¾ cup chopped nuts

1. Preheat oven to 350°F. In large bowl, combine all ingredients except candy bar pieces and nuts; beat until smooth.

2. Stir in remaining ingredients. Drop by rounded teaspoonfuls, 2 inches apart, onto ungreased baking sheets.

3. Bake 10 minutes or until tops are slightly crusted (do not overbake). Cool. Store tightly covered at room temperature.

Makes about 4½ dozen cookies

Prep Time: *15 minutes*
Bake Time: *10 minutes*

Mint Chocolate Cookies: Substitute ¾ cup mint-flavored chocolate chips for white chocolate candy bars with almonds. Proceed as directed above.

Peanut Blossom Cookies

1 (14-ounce) can EAGLE BRAND® Sweetened Condensed Milk (NOT evaporated milk)
¾ cup peanut butter
2 cups biscuit baking mix
1 teaspoon vanilla extract
⅓ cup sugar
60 solid milk chocolate candy kisses, unwrapped

1. Preheat oven to 375°F. In large bowl, beat EAGLE BRAND® and peanut butter until smooth. Add biscuit mix and vanilla; mix well. Shape into 1-inch balls. Roll in sugar. Place 2 inches apart on ungreased baking sheets.

2. Bake 6 to 8 minutes or until lightly browned (do not overbake). Remove from oven; immediately press candy kiss in center of each cookie. Cool. Store tightly covered at room temperature. *Makes about 5 dozen cookies*

Magic Make It Your Way
Drop Cookies

1. Preheat oven to 350°F. Grease baking sheets; set aside. In large bowl, sift together dry ingredients. Beat in butter, eggs, vanilla and EAGLE BRAND®. Fold in one "favorite" ingredient.

2. Drop by level teaspoonfuls, about 2 inches apart, onto prepared baking sheets. Bake 8 to 10 minutes or until edges are lightly browned. Immediately remove from baking sheet. Cool. Store covered at room temperature.

Makes about 4 dozen cookies

"Make it your way" with your favorite ingredient (pick one):

     1 (6-ounce) package semisweet chocolate chips
     1½ cups raisins
     1½ cups corn flakes
     1½ cups toasted flaked coconut

Prep Time: *15 minutes*
Bake Time: *8 to 10 minutes*

3 cups sifted all-purpose flour
3 teaspoons baking powder
¾ teaspoon salt
¾ cup (1½ sticks) butter or margarine, softened
2 eggs
1 teaspoon vanilla extract
1 (14-ounce) can EAGLE BRAND® Sweetened Condensed Milk (NOT evaporated milk)
One "favorite" ingredient

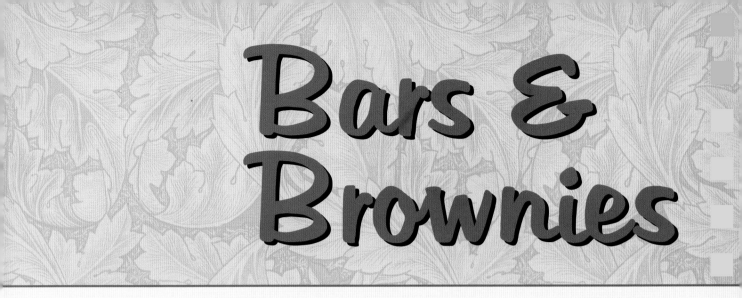

Bars & Brownies

Streusel Caramel Bars

2 cups all-purpose flour
¾ cup firmly packed light
    brown sugar
1 egg, beaten
¾ cup (1½ sticks) cold
    butter or margarine,
    divided
¾ cup chopped nuts
24 caramels, unwrapped
1 (14-ounce) can EAGLE
    BRAND® Sweetened
    Condensed Milk
    (NOT evaporated milk)

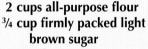

1. Preheat oven to 350°F. Grease 13×9-inch baking pan. In large bowl, combine flour, brown sugar and egg; cut in ½ cup butter until crumbly. Stir in nuts. Reserve 2 cups crumb mixture. Press remaining crumb mixture firmly on bottom of prepared pan. Bake 15 minutes.

2. Meanwhile, in heavy saucepan over low heat, melt caramels and remaining ¼ cup butter with EAGLE BRAND®. Pour evenly over baked crust. Top with reserved crumb mixture.

3. Bake 20 minutes or until bubbly. Cool. Cut into bars. Store loosely covered at room temperature. *Makes 2 to 3 dozen bars*

Prep Time: *25 minutes*
Bake Time: *35 minutes*

Pecan Pie Bars

2 cups all-purpose flour
¼ cup firmly packed brown sugar
½ cup (1 stick) butter
1½ cups chopped pecans
1 (14-ounce) can EAGLE BRAND® Sweetened Condensed Milk (NOT evaporated milk)
3 eggs, beaten
2 tablespoons lemon juice from concentrate

1. Preheat oven to 350°F. In medium bowl, combine flour and brown sugar; cut in butter until crumbly.

2. Press mixture on bottom of ungreased 13×9-inch baking pan. Bake 10 to 15 minutes or until crust is light golden.

3. In large bowl, combine pecans, EAGLE BRAND®, eggs and lemon juice. Pour evenly over baked crust.

4. Bake 25 minutes or until filling is set. Cool. Cut into bars. Store covered at room temperature. *Makes 3 dozen bars*

Bars & Brownies

S'More Bars

1. Preheat oven to 350°F (325°F for glass dish). In 13×9-inch baking pan, melt butter in oven.

2. Sprinkle graham cracker crumbs evenly over butter; pour EAGLE BRAND® evenly over crumbs. Sprinkle with chocolate chips and nuts (optional); press down gently with fork.

3. Bake 25 minutes. Remove from oven; sprinkle with marshmallows. Return to oven. Bake 2 minutes more. Cool. Chill, if desired. Cut into bars. Store covered at room temperature.　　　*Makes 2 to 3 dozen bars*

½ cup (1 stick) butter or margarine

1½ cups graham cracker crumbs

1 (14-ounce) can EAGLE BRAND® Sweetened Condensed Milk (NOT evaporated milk)

1 cup (6 ounces) milk chocolate or semisweet chocolate chips

1 cup chopped nuts (optional)

1 cup miniature marshmallows

Bars & Brownies

Chocolate Cranberry Bars

2 cups vanilla wafer
   crumbs
½ cup unsweetened cocoa
3 tablespoons sugar
⅔ cup (1⅓ sticks) cold
   butter, cut into pieces
1 (14-ounce) can EAGLE
   BRAND® Sweetened
   Condensed Milk
   (NOT evaporated milk)
1⅓ cups (6-ounce package)
   sweetened dried
   cranberries or raisins
1 cup peanut butter-
   flavored chips
1 cup finely chopped
   walnuts

1. Preheat oven to 350°F. In medium bowl, combine wafer crumbs, cocoa and sugar; cut in butter until crumbly.

2. Press mixture evenly on bottom and ½ inch up sides of ungreased 13×9-inch baking pan. Pour EAGLE BRAND® evenly over crumb mixture. Sprinkle evenly with dried cranberries, peanut butter chips and walnuts; press down firmly.

3. Bake 25 to 30 minutes or until lightly browned. Cool completely in pan on wire rack. Cover with foil; let stand several hours. Cut into bars. Store covered at room temperature. *Makes 3 dozen bars*

Prep Time: *15 minutes*
Bake Time: *25 to 30 minutes*

Brownie Raspberry Bars

1. Preheat oven to 350°F. In heavy saucepan over low heat, melt chocolate chips with butter.

2. In large bowl, combine chocolate mixture, biscuit mix, EAGLE BRAND®, egg and vanilla; mix well. Stir in nuts. Spread in well-greased 15×10×1-inch baking pan. Bake 20 minutes or until center is set. Cool completely.

3. In small bowl, beat cream cheese, powdered sugar, jam and food coloring (optional) until smooth; spread over brownies. Garnish with Chocolate Drizzle. Chill. Cut into bars. Store leftovers covered in refrigerator.

Makes 3 to 4 dozen bars

Chocolate Drizzle: In heavy saucepan over low heat, melt ½ cup semisweet chocolate chips with 1 tablespoon shortening. Immediately drizzle over bars.

1 cup (6 ounces) semisweet chocolate chips
¼ cup (½ stick) butter
2 cups biscuit baking mix
1 (14-ounce) can EAGLE BRAND® Sweetened Condensed Milk (NOT evaporated milk)
1 egg
1 teaspoon vanilla extract
1 cup chopped nuts
1 (8-ounce) package cream cheese, softened
½ cup powdered sugar
½ cup red raspberry jam
Red food coloring (optional)
Chocolate Drizzle (recipe follows)

Candy Bar Bars

¾ cup (1½ sticks) butter or margarine, softened
¼ cup peanut butter
1 cup firmly packed light brown sugar
1 teaspoon baking soda
2 cups quick-cooking oats
1½ cups all-purpose flour
1 egg
1 (14-ounce) can EAGLE BRAND® Sweetened Condensed Milk (NOT evaporated milk)
4 cups chopped candy bars

1. Preheat oven to 350°F. In large bowl, combine butter and peanut butter. Add brown sugar and baking soda; beat well. Stir in oats and flour. Reserve 1¾ cups crumb mixture.

2. Stir egg into remaining crumb mixture; press firmly on bottom of ungreased 15×10×1-inch baking pan. Bake 15 minutes.

3. Pour EAGLE BRAND® evenly over baked crust. Stir together reserved crumb mixture and candy bar pieces; sprinkle evenly over top. Bake 25 minutes or until golden. Cool. Cut into bars. Store covered at room temperature.
Makes 4 dozen bars

Prep Time: *20 minutes*
Bake Time: *40 minutes*

Tip: For this recipe, use your favorite candy bars, such as chocolate-covered caramel-topped nougat bars with peanuts, chocolate-covered crisp wafers, chocolate-covered caramel-topped cookie bars or chocolate-covered peanut butter cups.

Bars & Brownies

Brownie Mint Sundae Squares

1. Line 13×9-inch baking pan with foil; grease. Prepare brownie mix as package directs; stir in walnuts. Spread in prepared pan. Bake as directed. Cool completely.

2. In large bowl, combine EAGLE BRAND®, peppermint extract and food coloring (optional). Fold in whipped cream and chocolate chips. Pour over brownie layer.

3. Cover; freeze 6 hours or until firm. To serve, lift brownies from pan with foil; cut into squares. Serve with hot fudge sauce (optional). Freeze leftovers.

Makes 10 to 12 servings

1 (19.5- or 19.8-ounce family-size) package fudge brownie mix, plus ingredients to prepare mix

¾ cup coarsely chopped walnuts

1 (14-ounce) can EAGLE BRAND® Sweetened Condensed Milk (NOT evaporated milk)

2 teaspoons peppermint extract

4 to 6 drops green food coloring (optional)

2 cups (1 pint) whipping cream, whipped

½ cup miniature semisweet chocolate chips

Hot fudge sauce or chocolate-flavored syrup (optional)

Double Delicious Cookie Bars

½ cup (1 stick) butter or margarine

1½ cups graham cracker crumbs

1 (14-ounce) can EAGLE BRAND® Sweetened Condensed Milk (NOT evaporated milk)

1 cup (6 ounces) semisweet chocolate chips*

1 cup (6 ounces) peanut butter-flavored chips*

*Butterscotch-flavored chips or white chocolate chips can be substituted for the semisweet chocolate chips and/or the peanut butter-flavored chips.

1. Preheat oven to 350°F (325°F for glass dish). In 13×9-inch baking pan, melt butter in oven.

2. Sprinkle graham cracker crumbs evenly over butter; pour EAGLE BRAND® evenly over crumbs. Top with remaining ingredients; press down firmly.

3. Bake 25 to 30 minutes or until lightly browned. Cool. Cut into bars. Store covered at room temperature.   *Makes 2 to 3 dozen bars*

Prep Time: *10 minutes*
Bake Time: *25 to 30 minutes*

Bars & Brownies

Fudge-Filled Bars

1. Preheat oven to 350°F. In heavy saucepan over medium heat, melt chocolate chips and butter with EAGLE BRAND®, stirring often. Remove from heat; stir in vanilla. Cool 15 minutes.

2. Using floured hands, press 1½ packages of cookie dough into ungreased 15×10×1-inch baking pan. Pour cooled chocolate mixture evenly over dough. Crumble remaining dough over chocolate mixture.

3. Bake 25 to 30 minutes. Cool. Cut into bars. Store covered at room temperature.

Makes 4 dozen bars

Prep Time: *20 minutes*
Bake Time: *25 to 30 minutes*

Helpful Hint: If you want to trim the fat in any EAGLE BRAND® recipe, just use EAGLE BRAND® Fat Free or Low Fat Sweetened Condensed Milk instead of the original EAGLE BRAND®.

1 (12-ounce) package semisweet chocolate chips
2 tablespoons butter or margarine
1 (14-ounce) can EAGLE BRAND® Sweetened Condensed Milk (NOT evaporated milk)
2 teaspoons vanilla extract
2 (18-ounce) packages refrigerated cookie dough (oatmeal-chocolate chip, chocolate chip or sugar cookie dough)

White Chocolate Squares

1 (12-ounce) package
    white chocolate chips,
    divided
¼ cup (½ stick) butter or
    margarine
1 (14-ounce) can EAGLE
    BRAND® Sweetened
    Condensed Milk
    (NOT evaporated milk)
1 egg
1 teaspoon vanilla extract
2 cups all-purpose flour
½ teaspoon baking powder
1 cup chopped pecans,
    toasted
    Powdered sugar

1. Preheat oven to 350°F. Grease 13×9-inch baking pan. In large saucepan over low heat, melt 1 cup white chocolate chips and butter. Stir in EAGLE BRAND®, egg and vanilla. Stir in flour and baking powder until blended. Stir in pecans and remaining white chocolate chips. Spoon mixture into prepared pan.

2. Bake 20 to 25 minutes. Cool. Sprinkle with powdered sugar; cut into squares. Store covered at room temperature. *Makes 2 dozen squares*

Prep Time: *15 minutes*
Bake Time: *20 to 25 minutes*

Bars & Brownies

Granola Bars

1. Preheat oven to 325°F. Line 15×10×1-inch baking pan with foil; grease.

2. In large bowl, combine all ingredients; mix well. Press evenly into prepared pan.

3. Bake 25 to 30 minutes or until golden brown. Cool slightly; remove from pan and peel off foil. Cut into bars. Store loosely covered at room temperature.

Makes 4 dozen bars

Prep Time: *20 minutes*
Bake Time: *25 to 30 minutes*

3 cups oats
1 (14-ounce) can EAGLE BRAND® Sweetened Condensed Milk (NOT evaporated milk)
1 cup peanuts
1 cup sunflower seeds
1 cup raisins
½ cup (1 stick) butter or margarine, melted
1½ teaspoons ground cinnamon

Chocolate Fantasy Bars

1 (18.25- or 18.5-ounce)
  package chocolate
  cake mix
⅓ cup vegetable oil
1 egg
1 cup chopped nuts
1 cup (6 ounces) semisweet
  chocolate chips
1 (14-ounce) can EAGLE
  BRAND® Sweetened
  Condensed Milk
  (NOT evaporated milk)
1 teaspoon vanilla extract
  Dash salt
1 tube decorating icing
  (optional)

1. Preheat oven to 350°F. In large bowl with mixer on medium speed, beat cake mix, oil and egg until crumbly. Stir in nuts. Reserve 1 cup crumb mixture. Firmly press remaining crumb mixture on bottom of greased 13×9-inch baking pan.

2. In small saucepan over low heat, melt chocolate chips with EAGLE BRAND®, vanilla and salt. Pour evenly over prepared crust. Sprinkle reserved crumb mixture evenly over top. Bake 25 to 30 minutes or until edges are firm. Cool. Cut into bars. Drizzle with icing (optional). Store loosely covered at room temperature.   *Makes 2 to 3 dozen bars*

Chewy Almond Squares

1¼ cups graham cracker
  crumbs
¼ cup sugar
⅓ cup (⅔ stick) butter or
  margarine, melted
1 cup flaked coconut,
  toasted
1 cup chopped almonds,
  toasted*
1 (14-ounce) can EAGLE
  BRAND® Sweetened
  Condensed Milk
  (NOT evaporated milk)

1 cup chopped pecans or walnuts, toasted, can be substituted.

1. Preheat oven to 375°F. Line 9-inch square baking pan with foil. In medium bowl, combine graham cracker crumbs, sugar and butter. Press firmly on bottom of prepared pan. Bake 5 to 7 minutes.

2. Sprinkle baked crust with coconut and almonds; pour EAGLE BRAND® evenly over top.

3. Bake 25 to 30 minutes. Cool on wire rack. Cut into squares. Store covered at room temperature.   *Makes 16 squares*

Prep Time: *10 minutes*
Bake Time: *30 to 37 minutes*

Bars & Brownies

Chocolate & Almond Bars

1. Preheat oven to 350°F. In large bowl, combine flour and sugar; cut in butter until crumbly. Press firmly on bottom of ungreased 13×9-inch baking pan. Bake 20 minutes or until lightly browned.

2. In medium saucepan over low heat, melt 1 cup chocolate chips with EAGLE BRAND®. Remove from heat; cool slightly. Beat in egg. Stir in almonds and extract. Spread over baked crust. Bake 25 minutes or until set. Cool.

3. Melt remaining ½ cup chocolate chips with shortening; drizzle over bars. Chill 10 minutes or until set. Cut into bars. Store covered at room temperature.

Makes about 2 dozen bars

1½ cups all-purpose flour
⅔ cup sugar
¾ cup (1½ sticks) cold butter or margarine
1½ cups semisweet chocolate chips, divided
1 (14-ounce) can EAGLE BRAND® Sweetened Condensed Milk (NOT evaporated milk)
1 egg
2 cups almonds, toasted and chopped
½ teaspoon almond extract
1 teaspoon solid shortening

Bars & Brownies

Harvest Apple Streusel Squares

2 cups graham cracker crumbs

¾ cup (1½ sticks) butter or margarine, melted

½ cup finely chopped pecans

1 (8-ounce) package cream cheese, softened

1 (14-ounce) can EAGLE BRAND® Sweetened Condensed Milk (NOT evaporated milk)

2 eggs

1 (21-ounce) can apple pie filling

½ cup firmly packed brown sugar

½ cup all-purpose flour

¼ teaspoon ground cinnamon

¼ cup (½ stick) cold butter or margarine

½ cup dried cranberries

⅓ cup chopped pecans

1. Preheat oven to 350°F. In small bowl, combine graham cracker crumbs, butter and finely chopped pecans. Press evenly into parchment-paper-lined 13×9-inch baking pan.

2. In medium bowl, beat cream cheese until fluffy. Beat in EAGLE BRAND® and eggs. Pour over prepared crust. Spoon apple pie filling over cream cheese layer.

3. In another medium bowl, combine brown sugar, flour and cinnamon. Cut in cold butter until mixture resembles coarse crumbs. Stir in cranberries and chopped pecans. Sprinkle over apple layer. Bake 35 to 40 minutes or until golden (do not overbake).   *Makes 1 dozen squares*

Bars & Brownies

Cheesecake-Topped Brownies

1. Preheat oven to 350°F. Prepare brownie mix as package directs. Spread into well-greased 13×9-inch baking pan.

2. In large bowl, beat cream cheese, butter and cornstarch until fluffy.

3. Gradually beat in EAGLE BRAND®. Add egg and vanilla; beat until smooth. Pour cheesecake mixture evenly over brownie batter.

4. Bake 40 to 45 minutes or until top is lightly browned. Cool. Spread with frosting or sprinkle with orange peel (optional). Cut into bars. Store leftovers covered in refrigerator.   *Makes 3 to 3½ dozen brownies*

Prep Time: *20 minutes*
Bake Time: *40 to 45 minutes*

- 1 (19.5- or 19.8-ounce family-size) package fudge brownie mix, plus ingredients to prepare mix
- 1 (8-ounce) package cream cheese, softened
- 2 tablespoons butter or margarine, softened
- 1 tablespoon cornstarch
- 1 (14-ounce) can EAGLE BRAND® Sweetened Condensed Milk (NOT evaporated milk)
- 1 egg
- 2 teaspoons vanilla extract
  Ready-to-spread chocolate frosting (optional)
  Orange peel (optional)

Chocolate Nut Bars

1¾ cups graham cracker
    crumbs
½ cup (1 stick) butter or
    margarine, melted
2 cups (12 ounces)
    semisweet chocolate
    chips, divided
1 (14-ounce) can EAGLE
    BRAND® Sweetened
    Condensed Milk
    (NOT evaporated milk)
1 teaspoon vanilla extract
1 cup chopped nuts

1. Preheat oven to 375°F. In medium bowl, combine graham cracker crumbs and butter; press firmly on bottom of ungreased 13×9-inch baking pan. Bake 8 minutes. Reduce oven temperature to 350°F.

2. In small saucepan over low heat, melt 1 cup chocolate chips with EAGLE BRAND® and vanilla. Spread chocolate mixture over baked crust. Top with remaining 1 cup chocolate chips and nuts; press down firmly.

3. Bake 25 to 30 minutes. Cool. Chill, if desired. Cut into bars. Store loosely covered at room temperature. *Makes 2 to 3 dozen bars*

Prep Time: *10 minutes*
Bake Time: *33 to 38 minutes*

Golden Peanut Butter Bars

1. Preheat oven to 350°F. In large bowl, combine flour, brown sugar and egg; cut in cold butter until crumbly. Stir in peanuts. Reserve 2 cups crumb mixture. Press remaining mixture on bottom of ungreased 13×9-inch baking pan. Bake 15 minutes or until lightly browned.

2. Meanwhile, in another large bowl, beat EAGLE BRAND®, peanut butter and vanilla. Spread over baked crust; top with reserved crumb mixture.

3. Bake 25 minutes or until lightly browned. Cool. Cut into bars. Store covered at room temperature. *Makes 2 to 3 dozen bars*

Prep Time: *20 minutes*
Bake Time: *40 minutes*

2 cups all-purpose flour
¾ cup firmly packed light brown sugar
1 egg, beaten
½ cup (1 stick) cold butter or margarine
1 cup finely chopped peanuts
1 (14-ounce) can EAGLE BRAND® Sweetened Condensed Milk (NOT evaporated milk)
½ cup peanut butter
1 teaspoon vanilla extract

Fudgy Chocolate Pecan Bars

1 cup all-purpose flour
⅔ cup sugar
½ cup unsweetened cocoa
½ teaspoon salt
¾ cup (1½ sticks) cold
    butter or margarine
2 eggs, divided
1 (14-ounce) can EAGLE
    BRAND® Sweetened
    Condensed Milk
    (NOT evaporated milk)
1½ teaspoons maple
    flavoring
2 cups pecan halves or
    pieces

1. Preheat oven to 350°F. In large bowl, combine flour, sugar, cocoa and salt; cut in butter until crumbly. Stir in 1 beaten egg. Press firmly on bottom of ungreased 13×9-inch baking pan. Bake 25 minutes.

2. Meanwhile, in medium bowl, beat EAGLE BRAND®, remaining 1 egg and maple flavoring; stir in pecans. Pour over baked crust, distributing pecans evenly.

3. Bake 25 minutes or until golden. Cut into bars. Store tightly covered at room temperature. *Makes 2 to 3 dozen bars*

Prep Time: *20 minutes*
Bake Time: *50 minutes*

Double Chocolate Brownies

1¼ cups all-purpose flour,
    divided
¼ cup sugar
½ cup (1 stick) cold butter
    or margarine
1 (14-ounce) can EAGLE
    BRAND® Sweetened
    Condensed Milk
    (NOT evaporated milk)
¼ cup unsweetened cocoa
1 egg
1 teaspoon vanilla extract
½ teaspoon baking powder
1 (8-ounce) milk chocolate
    candy bar, broken into
    chunks
¾ cup chopped nuts
    (optional)

1. Preheat oven to 350°F. Line 13×9-inch baking pan with foil; set aside.

2. In medium bowl, combine 1 cup flour and sugar; cut in butter until crumbly. Press firmly on bottom of prepared pan. Bake 15 minutes.

3. In large bowl, beat EAGLE BRAND®, cocoa, egg, remaining ¼ cup flour, vanilla and baking powder. Stir in candy bar chunks and nuts (optional). Spread over baked crust.

4. Bake 20 minutes or until set. Cool. Use foil to lift out of pan. Cut into bars. Store tightly covered at room temperature. *Makes 2 dozen brownies*

Prep Time: *15 minutes*
Bake Time: *35 minutes*

Magic Cookie Bars

1. Preheat oven to 350°F (325°F for glass dish). In 13×9-inch baking pan, melt butter in oven.

2. Sprinkle graham cracker crumbs evenly over butter; pour EAGLE BRAND® evenly over crumbs. Layer evenly with remaining ingredients; press down firmly.

3. Bake 25 minutes or until lightly browned. Cool. Cut into bars. Store loosely covered at room temperature.
Makes 2 to 3 dozen bars

Prep Time: *10 minutes*
Bake Time: *25 minutes*

7-Layer Magic Cookie Bars: Substitute 1 cup (6 ounces) butterscotch-flavored chips for 1 cup semisweet chocolate chips. (Peanut butter-flavored chips or white chocolate chips can be substituted for butterscotch-flavored chips.)

Magic Peanut Cookie Bars: Substitute 2 cups (about ¾ pound) chocolate-covered peanuts for semisweet chocolate chips and chopped nuts.

Magic Rainbow Cookie Bars: Substitute 2 cups plain candy-coated chocolate pieces for semisweet chocolate chips.

½ cup (1 stick) butter or margarine
1½ cups graham cracker crumbs
1 (14-ounce) can EAGLE BRAND® Sweetened Condensed Milk (NOT evaporated milk)
2 cups (12 ounces) semisweet chocolate chips
1⅓ cups flaked coconut
1 cup chopped nuts

Fudge Topped Brownies

2 cups sugar
1 cup (2 sticks) butter or
    margarine, melted
1 cup all-purpose flour
⅔ cup unsweetened cocoa
½ teaspoon baking powder
2 eggs
½ cup milk
3 teaspoons vanilla extract,
    divided
1 cup chopped nuts
    (optional)
2 cups (12 ounces)
    semisweet chocolate
    chips
1 (14-ounce) can EAGLE
    BRAND® Sweetened
    Condensed Milk
    (NOT evaporated milk)
Dash salt

1. Preheat oven to 350°F. In large bowl, combine sugar, butter, flour, cocoa, baking powder, eggs, milk and 1½ teaspoons vanilla; mix well. Stir in nuts (optional). Spread in greased 13×9-inch baking pan. Bake 40 minutes or until brownies begin to pull away from sides of pan.

2. Meanwhile, in heavy saucepan over low heat, melt chocolate chips with EAGLE BRAND®, remaining 1½ teaspoons vanilla and salt. Remove from heat. Immediately spread over hot brownies. Cool. Chill. Cut into bars. Store covered at room temperature. *Makes 3 to 3½ dozen brownies*

Bars & Brownies

Butterscotch Apple Squares

1. Preheat oven to 350°F (325°F for glass dish). In 13×9-inch baking pan, melt butter in oven. Sprinkle graham cracker crumbs evenly over butter; top with apples.

2. In heavy saucepan over medium heat, melt butterscotch chips with EAGLE BRAND®. Pour butterscotch mixture evenly over apples. Top with coconut and nuts; press down firmly.

3. Bake 25 to 30 minutes or until lightly browned. Cool. Cut into squares. Store covered in refrigerator.   *Makes 1 dozen squares*

Prep Time: *15 minutes*
Bake Time: *25 to 30 minutes*

¼ cup (½ stick) butter or margarine
1½ cups graham cracker crumbs
2 small all-purpose apples, peeled and chopped (about 1¼ cups)
1 (6-ounce) package butterscotch-flavored chips
1 (14-ounce) can EAGLE BRAND® Sweetened Condensed Milk (NOT evaporated milk)
1⅓ cups flaked coconut
1 cup chopped nuts

Bars & Brownies

No-Bake Fudgy Brownies

1 (14-ounce) can EAGLE BRAND® Sweetened Condensed Milk (NOT evaporated milk)

2 (1-ounce) squares unsweetened chocolate, chopped

1 teaspoon vanilla extract

2 cups plus 2 tablespoons packaged chocolate cookie crumbs, divided

¼ cup miniature candy-coated milk chocolate pieces or chopped nuts

1. Grease 8-inch square baking pan or line with foil; set aside.

2. In medium saucepan over low heat, combine EAGLE BRAND® and chocolate; cook and stir just until boiling. Reduce heat; cook and stir for 2 to 3 minutes more or until mixture thickens. Remove from heat; stir in vanilla.

3. Stir in 2 cups cookie crumbs. Spread evenly in prepared pan. Sprinkle with remaining cookie crumbs and chocolate pieces or nuts; press down gently with back of spoon.

4. Cover and chill 4 hours or until firm. Cut into squares. Store leftovers covered in refrigerator. *Makes 2 to 3 dozen bars*

Prep Time: *10 minutes*
Chill Time: *4 hours*

Lemon Crumb Bars

1. Preheat oven to 350°F. Grease 15×10×1-inch baking pan. In large bowl, combine cake mix, butter and 1 egg; mix well. (Mixture will be crumbly.) Stir in cracker crumbs. Reserve 2 cups crumb mixture. Press remaining crumb mixture firmly on bottom of prepared pan. Bake 15 minutes.

2. Meanwhile, in medium bowl, combine EAGLE BRAND®, lemon juice and egg yolks; mix well. Spread evenly over baked crust.

3. Top with reserved crumb mixture. Bake 20 minutes or until firm. Cool. Cut into bars. Store covered in refrigerator. *Makes 3 to 4 dozen bars*

Prep Time: *30 minutes*
Bake Time: *35 minutes*

1 (18.25-ounce) package lemon or yellow cake mix
½ cup (1 stick) butter or margarine, softened
1 egg
2 cups finely crushed saltine cracker crumbs
1 (14-ounce) can EAGLE BRAND® Sweetened Condensed Milk (NOT evaporated milk)
½ cup lemon juice from concentrate
3 egg yolks

Toffee Bars

1 cup quick-cooking oats
½ cup all-purpose flour
½ cup firmly packed light brown sugar
½ cup finely chopped walnuts
½ cup (1 stick) butter or margarine, melted and divided
¼ teaspoon baking soda
1 (14-ounce) can EAGLE BRAND® Sweetened Condensed Milk (NOT evaporated milk)
2 teaspoons vanilla extract
2 cups (12 ounces) semisweet chocolate chips
Additional chopped walnuts (optional)

1. Preheat oven to 350°F. Grease 13×9-inch baking pan. In large bowl, combine oats, flour, brown sugar, walnuts, 6 tablespoons butter and baking soda. Press firmly on bottom of prepared pan. Bake 10 to 15 minutes or until lightly browned.

2. Meanwhile, in medium saucepan over medium heat, combine remaining 2 tablespoons butter and EAGLE BRAND®. Cook and stir until mixture thickens slightly, about 15 minutes. Remove from heat; stir in vanilla. Pour evenly over baked crust. Bake 10 to 15 minutes or until golden brown.

3. Remove from oven; immediately sprinkle with chocolate chips. Let stand 1 minute; spread chocolate chips while still warm. Garnish with additional walnuts (optional); press down firmly. Cool completely. Cut into bars. Store tightly covered at room temperature.　　　*Makes 3 dozen bars*

Cookie Pizza

1. Preheat oven to 375°F. Divide cookie dough in half; press each half onto ungreased 12-inch pizza pan. Bake 10 minutes or until golden.

2. In medium saucepan, melt chocolate chips with EAGLE BRAND®. Spread over crusts. Sprinkle with chocolate pieces, marshmallows and peanuts.

3. Bake 4 minutes or until marshmallows are lightly toasted. Cool. Cut into wedges.

Makes 2 pizzas (24 servings)

Prep Time: *15 minutes*
Bake Time: *14 minutes*

1 (18-ounce) package refrigerated sugar cookie dough

2 cups (12 ounces) semisweet chocolate chips

1 (14-ounce) can EAGLE BRAND® Sweetened Condensed Milk (NOT evaporated milk)

2 cups candy-coated milk chocolate pieces

2 cups miniature marshmallows

½ cup peanuts

Bars & Brownies

Cheesecakes

Chocolate Mint Cheesecake Bars

2 cups crushed chocolate
   wafer cookie crumbs
½ cup (1 stick) butter,
   melted
1 (8-ounce) package cream
   cheese, softened
1 (14-ounce) can EAGLE
   BRAND® Sweetened
   Condensed Milk
   (NOT evaporated milk)
2 eggs
1 tablespoon peppermint
   extract
1 cup (6 ounces) semisweet
   chocolate chips
6 ounces chocolate mint
   candies, chopped

1. Preheat oven to 325°F. In medium bowl, combine cookie crumbs and butter; blend well. Press firmly onto bottom of greased 13×9-inch baking pan. Bake 6 minutes. Cool.

2. In medium bowl, beat cream cheese until fluffy. Gradually beat in EAGLE BRAND®, eggs and peppermint extract until smooth. Pour over cooled crust; bake 25 to 30 minutes. Cool completely.

3. In heavy saucepan over low heat, melt chocolate chips; drizzle over bars. Sprinkle with chopped candies. Cut into bars. Store leftovers covered in refrigerator.

Makes 1½ to 2 dozen bars

Lemony Cheesecake Bars

1½ cups graham cracker crumbs
⅓ cup sugar
⅓ cup finely chopped pecans
⅓ cup (⅔ stick) butter or margarine, melted
2 (8-ounce) packages cream cheese, softened
1 (14-ounce) can EAGLE BRAND® Sweetened Condensed Milk (NOT evaporated milk)
2 eggs
½ cup lemon juice from concentrate

1. Preheat oven to 325°F. In medium bowl, combine graham cracker crumbs, sugar, pecans and butter. Reserve ⅓ cup crumb mixture; press remaining mixture firmly on bottom of ungreased 13×9-inch baking pan. Bake 5 minutes. Cool on wire rack.

2. In large bowl, beat cream cheese until fluffy. Gradually beat in EAGLE BRAND® until smooth. Add eggs; beat until just blended. Stir in lemon juice. Carefully spoon mixture into baked crust. Spoon reserved crumb mixture to make diagonal stripes on top of cheese mixture or sprinkle to cover.

3. Bake about 30 minutes or until knife inserted near center comes out clean. Cool on wire rack 1 hour. Cut into bars to serve. Store covered in refrigerator.

Makes 3 dozen bars

Prep Time: *25 minutes*
Bake Time: *35 minutes*
Cool Time: *1 hour*

Black & White Cheesecake

1. Preheat oven to 350°F. In medium bowl, beat cream cheese until fluffy. Gradually beat in EAGLE BRAND® until smooth. Add egg and vanilla; mix well.

2. In small bowl, toss chocolate chips with flour to coat; stir into cream cheese mixture. Pour into crust.

3. Bake 35 minutes or until center springs back when lightly touched. Cool. Prepare Chocolate Glaze and spread over cheesecake. Serve chilled. Store covered in refrigerator.   *Makes 6 to 8 servings*

Chocolate Glaze: In small saucepan over low heat, melt ½ cup miniature semisweet chocolate chips with ¼ cup whipping cream. Cook and stir until thickened and smooth. Use immediately.

Prep Time: *15 minutes*
Bake Time: *35 minutes*

2 (3-ounce) packages
   cream cheese, softened
1 (14-ounce) can EAGLE
   BRAND® Sweetened
   Condensed Milk
   (NOT evaporated milk)
1 egg
1 teaspoon vanilla extract
½ cup miniature semisweet
   chocolate chips
1 teaspoon all-purpose
   flour
1 (6-ounce) chocolate
   crumb crust
   Chocolate Glaze (recipe
   follows)

Maple Pumpkin Cheesecake

1¼ cups graham cracker
    crumbs
¼ cup sugar
¼ cup (½ stick) butter or
    margarine, melted
3 (8-ounce) packages
    cream cheese, softened
1 (14-ounce) can EAGLE
    BRAND® Sweetened
    Condensed Milk
    (NOT evaporated milk)
1 (15-ounce) can pumpkin
3 eggs
¼ cup maple syrup
1½ teaspoons ground
    cinnamon
1 teaspoon ground nutmeg
½ teaspoon salt
    Maple Pecan Glaze
    (recipe follows)

1. Preheat oven to 325°F. In small bowl, combine graham cracker crumbs, sugar and butter; press firmly on bottom of ungreased 9-inch springform pan.* In large bowl, beat cream cheese until fluffy. Gradually beat in EAGLE BRAND® until smooth. Add pumpkin, eggs, maple syrup, cinnamon, nutmeg and salt; mix well. Pour into prepared crust. Bake 1 hour 15 minutes or until center appears nearly set when shaken.

2. Cool 1 hour. Cover and chill at least 4 hours. Meanwhile, prepare Maple Pecan Glaze.

3. To serve, spoon some Maple Pecan Glaze over cheesecake. Garnish with whipped cream and pecans, if desired. Pass remaining glaze. Store leftovers covered in refrigerator.   *Makes 1 (9-inch) cheesecake*

*To use 13×9-inch baking pan, press crumb mixture firmly on bottom of pan. Proceed as directed, except bake 50 to 60 minutes or until center appears nearly set when shaken.

Maple Pecan Glaze: In medium saucepan over medium-high heat, combine 1 cup (½ pint) whipping cream and ¾ cup maple syrup; bring to a boil. Boil rapidly 15 to 20 minutes or until thickened, stirring occasionally. Stir in ½ cup chopped pecans.

Prep Time: *25 minutes*
Bake Time: *1 hour and 15 minutes*
Cool Time: *1 hour*
Chill Time: *4 hours*

Cheesecakes

Creamy Baked Cheesecake

1. Preheat oven to 300°F. In small bowl, combine graham cracker crumbs, sugar and butter; press firmly on bottom of ungreased 9-inch springform pan.

2. In large bowl, beat cream cheese until fluffy. Gradually beat in EAGLE BRAND® until smooth. Add eggs and lemon juice; mix well. Pour into prepared crust.

3. Bake 50 to 55 minutes or until set. Remove from oven; top with sour cream. Bake 5 minutes longer. Cool. Chill. Prepare Raspberry Topping (optional) and serve with cheesecake. Store covered in refrigerator.

Makes 1 (9-inch) cheesecake

Raspberry Topping

    1 (10-ounce) package thawed frozen red raspberries in syrup
    ¼ cup red currant jelly or red raspberry jam
    1 tablespoon cornstarch

1. Reserve ⅔ cup syrup from raspberries; set raspberries aside.

2. In small saucepan over medium heat, combine reserved syrup, jelly and cornstarch. Cook and stir until slightly thickened and clear. Cool. Stir in raspberries.

1¼ cups graham cracker
  crumbs
¼ cup sugar
⅓ cup (⅔ stick) butter or
  margarine, melted
2 (8-ounce) packages
  cream cheese, softened
1 (14-ounce) can EAGLE
  BRAND® Sweetened
  Condensed Milk
  (NOT evaporated milk)
3 eggs
¼ cup lemon juice from
  concentrate
1 (8-ounce) container sour
  cream, at room
  temperature
  Raspberry Topping
  (recipe follows,
  optional)

Espresso Cheesecake

1 cup graham cracker
   crumbs
1 cup plus 2 tablespoons
   sugar, divided
¼ cup (½ stick) butter or
   margarine, melted
1 cup water
¼ cup ground espresso
8 (1-ounce) squares
   semisweet chocolate
1 (14-ounce) can EAGLE
   BRAND® Sweetened
   Condensed Milk
   (NOT evaporated
   milk), divided
3 (8-ounce) packages
   cream cheese, softened
3 large eggs
¾ cup sour cream
1 tablespoon coffee liqueur
   Garnishes: whipped
   cream, chocolate-
   covered coffee beans

1. Preheat oven to 350°F. In medium bowl, combine graham cracker crumbs, 2 tablespoons sugar and butter. Press mixture firmly on bottom of ungreased 9-inch springform pan; set aside.

2. In small saucepan over high heat, bring 1 cup water to a boil. Add espresso; reduce heat to medium and simmer 1 minute. Pour through fine wire-mesh strainer into small bowl; discard grounds. Reserve 9 tablespoons coffee; discard remaining coffee.

3. In microwave-safe bowl, combine 7 tablespoons coffee, chocolate and ⅓ cup EAGLE BRAND®. Microwave at HIGH (100% power) 1 to 1½ minutes or until chocolate melts. Stir until smooth. Set aside.

4. In medium bowl, beat cream cheese and remaining 1 cup sugar until fluffy. Add eggs, 1 at a time, beating just until blended. Stir in chocolate mixture and sour cream. Pour into prepared crust.

5. Bake 45 minutes. Turn oven off and gently run knife around edge of pan to release side. Let stand in oven with door partially open 1 hour. Remove from oven. Cover and chill.

6. In small bowl, combine remaining EAGLE BRAND®, remaining 2 tablespoons coffee and liqueur. Serve with cake. Garnish, if desired.

Makes 1 (9-inch) cheesecake

Prep Time: *15 minutes*
Bake Time: *45 minutes*

Festive Cranberry Cheese Squares

1. Preheat oven to 350°F. Grease 13×9-inch baking pan. In large bowl, beat flour, oats, butter and ¾ cup brown sugar until crumbly. Reserve 1½ cups crumb mixture. Press remaining crumb mixture firmly on bottom of prepared pan. Bake 15 minutes or until lightly browned.

2. Meanwhile, in medium bowl, beat cream cheese until fluffy. Gradually beat in EAGLE BRAND® until smooth; stir in lemon juice. Spread over baked crust. In another medium bowl, combine cranberry sauce, cornstarch and remaining 1 tablespoon brown sugar. Spoon over cheese layer. Top with reserved crumb mixture.

3. Bake 45 minutes or until golden. Cool and cut into bars. Store covered in refrigerator.   *Makes 2 to 3 dozen squares*

Prep Time: *25 minutes*
Bake Time: *60 minutes*

Tip: Cut into large squares. Serve warm and top with ice cream.

2 cups all-purpose flour
1½ cups oats
1 cup (2 sticks) butter or margarine, softened
¾ cup plus 1 tablespoon firmly packed light brown sugar, divided
1 (8-ounce) package cream cheese, softened
1 (14-ounce) can EAGLE BRAND® Sweetened Condensed Milk (NOT evaporated milk)
¼ cup lemon juice from concentrate
1 (16-ounce) can whole berry cranberry sauce
2 tablespoons cornstarch

Frozen Peppermint Cheesecake

2 cups chocolate wafer cookie or sandwich cookie crumbs, divided
¼ cup sugar
¼ cup (½ stick) butter or margarine, melted
1 (8-ounce) package cream cheese, softened
1 (14-ounce) can EAGLE BRAND® Sweetened Condensed Milk (NOT evaporated milk)
2 teaspoons peppermint extract
Red food coloring (optional)
2 cups whipping cream, whipped
Fudge ice cream topping (optional)

1. Line 9-inch round cake or springform pan with foil. In medium bowl, combine cookie crumbs, sugar and butter; mix well. Press 2 cups crumb mixture firmly on bottom and halfway up side of prepared pan. Chill.

2. In large bowl, beat cream cheese until fluffy. Gradually beat in EAGLE BRAND® until smooth. Stir in peppermint extract and food coloring (optional); mix well. Fold in whipped cream. Pour into prepared crust. Cover; freeze 6 hours or until firm. Garnish with topping (optional). Store leftovers covered in freezer.

Makes 1 (9-inch) cheesecake

Cheesecakes

Mini Cheesecakes

1. Preheat oven to 300°F. In small bowl, combine graham cracker crumbs, sugar and butter; press equal portions firmly on bottoms of 24 lightly greased or paper-lined muffin cups.

2. In large bowl, beat cream cheese until fluffy. Gradually beat in EAGLE BRAND® until smooth. Add eggs and vanilla; mix well. Spoon equal amounts of mixture (about 3 tablespoons) into prepared cups. Bake 20 minutes or until cakes spring back when lightly touched. Cool.* Chill. Garnish as desired. Store leftovers covered in refrigerator.   *Makes 2 dozen mini cheesecakes*

If greased muffin cups are used, cool baked cheesecakes. Freeze 15 minutes; remove with narrow spatula. Proceed as directed above.

Prep Time: *20 minutes*
Bake Time: *20 minutes*

Chocolate Mini Cheesecakes: Melt 1 cup (6 ounces) semisweet chocolate chips; mix into batter. Proceed as directed above, baking 20 to 25 minutes.

1½ cups graham cracker or chocolate wafer cookie crumbs
¼ cup sugar
¼ cup (½ stick) butter or margarine, melted
3 (8-ounce) packages cream cheese, softened
1 (14-ounce) can EAGLE BRAND® Sweetened Condensed Milk (NOT evaporated milk)
3 eggs
2 teaspoons vanilla extract

Cheesecakes

Black Forest Chocolate Cheesecake

1½ cups chocolate cookie
crumbs

3 tablespoons butter or
margarine, melted

2 (1-ounce) squares
unsweetened
chocolate

1 (14-ounce) can EAGLE
BRAND® Sweetened
Condensed Milk
(NOT evaporated milk)

2 (8-ounce) packages
cream cheese, softened

3 eggs

3 tablespoons cornstarch

1 teaspoon almond extract

1 (21-ounce) can cherry
pie filling, chilled

1. Preheat oven to 300°F. In small bowl, combine cookie crumbs and butter; press firmly on bottom of ungreased 9-inch springform pan.

2. In small saucepan over low heat, melt chocolate with EAGLE BRAND®, stirring constantly. Remove from heat.

3. In large bowl, beat cream cheese until fluffy. Gradually add EAGLE BRAND® mixture until smooth. Add eggs, cornstarch and almond extract; mix well. Pour into prepared crust.

4. Bake 55 minutes or until center is almost set. Cool. Chill. Top with cherry pie filling before serving. Store leftovers covered in refrigerator.

Makes 1 (9-inch) cheesecake

Chocolate Chip Cheesecake

1. Preheat oven to 300°F. In small bowl, combine cookie crumbs and butter; press firmly on bottom of ungreased 9-inch springform pan.

2. In large bowl, beat cream cheese until fluffy. Gradually beat in EAGLE BRAND® until smooth. Add eggs and vanilla; mix well.

3. In small bowl, toss ½ cup chocolate chips with flour to coat; stir into cheese mixture. Pour into prepared crust. Sprinkle remaining ½ cup chocolate chips evenly over top.

4. Bake 55 to 60 minutes or until set. Cool. Chill. Garnish as desired. Store leftovers covered in refrigerator.   *Makes 1 (9-inch) cheesecake*

Tip: For the best distribution of the chocolate chips throughout this cheesecake, do not oversoften or overbeat the cream cheese.

1½ cups finely crushed creme-filled chocolate or vanilla sandwich cookie crumbs

2 to 3 tablespoons butter or margarine, melted

3 (8-ounce) packages cream cheese, softened

1 (14-ounce) can EAGLE BRAND® Sweetened Condensed Milk (NOT evaporated milk)

3 eggs

2 teaspoons vanilla extract

1 cup miniature semisweet chocolate chips, divided

1 teaspoon all-purpose flour

Walnut Rum Raisin Cheesecake

1 cup raisins
2 tablespoons rum or water
plus ½ teaspoon rum
flavoring
1 cup graham cracker
crumbs
½ cup finely chopped
walnuts
¼ cup sugar
¼ cup (½ stick) butter or
margarine, melted
3 (8-ounce) packages
cream cheese, softened
1 (14-ounce) can EAGLE
BRAND® Sweetened
Condensed Milk
(NOT evaporated milk)
3 eggs
Walnut Praline Glaze
(recipe follows)

1. Preheat oven to 300°F. In small bowl, combine raisins and rum; set aside.

2. In medium bowl, combine graham cracker crumbs, walnuts, sugar and butter; press firmly on bottom of ungreased 9-inch springform pan or 13×9-inch baking pan.

3. In large bowl, beat cream cheese until fluffy. Gradually beat in EAGLE BRAND® until smooth. Add eggs; mix well. Stir rum from raisins into batter. Pour into prepared crust. Top evenly with raisins.

4. Bake 55 to 60 minutes or until center is set. Cool. Top with Walnut Praline Glaze. Chill. Store leftovers covered in refrigerator.

Makes 1 (9-inch) cheesecake

Walnut Praline Glaze: In small saucepan over medium heat, combine ⅓ cup firmly packed dark brown sugar and ⅓ cup whipping cream. Cook and stir until sugar dissolves. Bring to a boil; reduce heat and simmer 5 minutes or until thickened. Remove from heat; stir in ¾ cup chopped toasted walnuts. Spoon over cake. (For 13×9-inch pan, double all glaze ingredients; simmer 10 to 12 minutes or until thickened.)

Prep Time: *20 minutes*
Bake Time: *55 to 60 minutes*

Chocolate Streusel Bars

1¾ cups all-purpose flour
1½ cups powdered sugar
½ cup unsweetened cocoa
1 cup (2 sticks) cold butter
or margarine
1 (8-ounce) package cream
cheese, softened
1 (14-ounce) can EAGLE
BRAND® Sweetened
Condensed Milk
(NOT evaporated milk)
1 egg
2 teaspoons vanilla extract
½ cup chopped walnuts

1. Preheat oven to 350°F. In large bowl, combine flour, sugar and cocoa; cut in butter until crumbly (mixture will be dry). Reserve 2 cups crumb mixture. Press remaining crumb mixture firmly on bottom of ungreased 13×9-inch baking pan. Bake 15 minutes.

2. Meanwhile, in large bowl, beat cream cheese until fluffy. Gradually beat in EAGLE BRAND® until smooth. Add egg and vanilla; mix well. Pour evenly over baked crust.

3. Combine reserved crumb mixture and walnuts; sprinkle evenly over cheese mixture. Bake 25 minutes or until bubbly. Cool. Chill. Cut into bars. Store covered in refrigerator.

Makes 2 to 3 dozen bars

Prep Time: *15 minutes*
Bake Time: *40 minutes*

Raspberry Swirl Cheesecakes

1. Preheat oven to 350°F. In blender container, blend 1½ cups raspberries until smooth; press through sieve to remove seeds. Stir ⅓ cup EAGLE BRAND® into raspberry purée; set aside.

2. In large bowl, beat cream cheese, eggs and remaining EAGLE BRAND®. Spoon into crusts. Drizzle with raspberry mixture. With table knife, gently swirl raspberry mixture through cream cheese mixture.

3. Bake 25 minutes or until centers are nearly set when shaken. Cool; chill at least 4 hours. Garnish with chocolate leaves and fresh raspberries (optional). Store leftovers covered in refrigerator.

Makes 2 (8- or 9-inch) cheesecakes

Prep Time: *15 minutes*
Bake Time: *25 minutes*
Chill Time: *4 hours*

Chocolate Leaves: Place 1 (1-ounce) square semisweet or white chocolate in microwave-safe bowl. Microwave at HIGH (100% power) 1 to 2 minutes, stirring every minute until smooth. With small, clean paintbrush, paint several coats of melted chocolate on undersides of nontoxic leaves, such as mint, lemon or strawberry. Wipe off any chocolate from top sides of leaves. Place leaves, chocolate sides up, on wax-paper-lined baking sheet or on curved surface, such as rolling pin. Refrigerate leaves until chocolate is firm. To use, carefully peel leaves away from chocolate.

1½ cups fresh or thawed lightly sweetened loose-pack frozen red raspberries
1 (14-ounce) can EAGLE BRAND® Sweetened Condensed Milk (NOT evaporated milk), divided
2 (8-ounce) packages cream cheese, softened
3 eggs
2 (8- or 9-inch) prepared chocolate crumb crusts
Chocolate and white chocolate leaves (recipe follows, optional)
Fresh raspberries (optional)

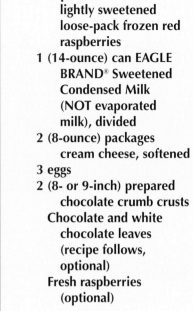

Pumpkin Cheesecake Bars

1 (16-ounce) package
    pound cake mix
3 eggs, divided
2 tablespoons butter or
    margarine, melted
4 teaspoons pumpkin pie
    spice, divided
1 (8-ounce) package cream
    cheese, softened
1 (14-ounce) can EAGLE
    BRAND® Sweetened
    Condensed Milk
    (NOT evaporated milk)
1 (15-ounce) can pumpkin
    (2 cups)
½ teaspoon salt
1 cup chopped nuts

1. Preheat oven to 350°F. In large bowl, beat cake mix, 1 egg, butter and 2 teaspoons pumpkin pie spice until crumbly. Press onto bottom of ungreased 15×10×1-inch baking pan.

2. In large bowl, beat cream cheese until fluffy. Gradually beat in EAGLE BRAND® until smooth. Beat in remaining 2 eggs, pumpkin, remaining 2 teaspoons pumpkin pie spice and salt; mix well. Pour into prepared crust; sprinkle with nuts.

3. Bake 30 to 35 minutes or until set. Cool. Chill; cut into bars. Store leftovers covered in refrigerator. *Makes 4 dozen bars*

Microwave Cheesecake

1. In 10-inch microwave-safe quiche dish or pie plate, melt butter loosely covered at HIGH (100% power) 1 minute. Add graham cracker crumbs and sugar; press firmly on bottom of dish. Microwave at HIGH (100% power) 1½ minutes, rotating dish once.

2. In 2-quart glass measure, beat cream cheese until fluffy. Gradually beat in EAGLE BRAND® until smooth. Add eggs and lemon juice; mix well. Microwave at MEDIUM-HIGH (70% power) 6 to 8 minutes or until hot, stirring every 2 minutes. Pour into prepared crust.

3. Microwave at MEDIUM (50% power) 6 to 8 minutes or until center is set, rotating dish once. Top with sour cream. Cool. Chill 3 hours or until set. Serve or top with fruit, if desired. Store covered in refrigerator.

Makes 1 (10-inch) cheesecake

Prep Time: *15 minutes*
Cook Time: *14½ to 18½ minutes*
Chill Time: *3 hours*

⅓ cup (⅔ stick) butter or margarine
1¼ cups graham cracker crumbs
¼ cup sugar
2 (8-ounce) packages cream cheese, softened
1 (14-ounce) can EAGLE BRAND® Sweetened Condensed Milk (NOT evaporated milk)
3 eggs
¼ cup lemon juice from concentrate
1 (8-ounce) container sour cream, at room temperature

Cheesecakes

Frozen Mocha Cheesecake Loaf

2 cups finely crushed creme-filled chocolate sandwich cookies (about 20 cookies)

3 tablespoons butter or margarine, melted

1 (8-ounce) package cream cheese, softened

1 (14-ounce) can EAGLE BRAND® Sweetened Condensed Milk (NOT evaporated milk)

1 tablespoon vanilla extract

2 cups (1 pint) whipping cream, whipped

2 tablespoons instant coffee dissolved in 1 tablespoon hot water

½ cup chocolate-flavored syrup

1. Line 9×5-inch loaf pan with foil, extending foil over sides of pan. In small bowl, combine cookie crumbs and butter; press firmly on bottom and halfway up sides of prepared pan.

2. In large bowl, beat cream cheese until fluffy. Gradually add EAGLE BRAND® until smooth; add vanilla. Fold in whipped cream.

3. Remove half the mixture and place in medium bowl; fold in coffee mixture and chocolate syrup. Spoon half the chocolate mixture into prepared crust, then half the vanilla mixture. Repeat. With table knife, cut through cream mixture to marble.

4. Cover; freeze 6 hours or until firm. To serve, remove from pan; peel off foil. Cut into slices and garnish as desired. Store leftovers covered in freezer.

Makes 8 to 10 servings

Prep Time: *20 minutes*
Freeze Time: *6 hours*

Cheesecakes

Almond Praline Cheesecake

1. Preheat oven to 300°F. In medium bowl, combine graham cracker crumbs, almonds, brown sugar and butter; press on bottom of ungreased 9-inch springform pan or 13×9-inch baking pan.

2. In large bowl, beat cream cheese until fluffy. Gradually beat in EAGLE BRAND® until smooth. Add eggs and almond extract; mix well. Pour into prepared crust.

3. Bake 55 to 60 minutes or until center is set. Cool. Top with Almond Praline Topping. Chill. Store leftovers covered in refrigerator.

Makes 1 (9-inch) cheesecake

Almond Praline Topping

⅓ **cup firmly packed dark brown sugar**
⅓ **cup whipping cream**
½ **cup chopped toasted slivered almonds**

In small saucepan over medium heat, combine brown sugar and cream. Cook and stir until sugar dissolves. Simmer 5 minutes or until thickened. Remove from heat; add almonds. Spoon evenly over cake. (To make topping for 13×9-inch pan, double all topping ingredients; simmer 10 to 12 minutes or until thickened.)

¾ **cup graham cracker crumbs**
½ **cup slivered almonds, toasted and finely chopped**
¼ **cup firmly packed brown sugar**
¼ **cup (½ stick) butter or margarine, melted**
3 **(8-ounce) packages cream cheese, softened**
1 **(14-ounce) can EAGLE BRAND® Sweetened Condensed Milk (NOT evaporated milk)**
3 **eggs**
1 **teaspoon almond extract**
  Almond Praline Topping (recipe follows)

Toffee-Top Cheesecake Bars

1¼ cups all-purpose flour
1 cup powdered sugar
½ cup unsweetened cocoa
¼ teaspoon baking soda
¾ cup (1½ sticks) butter or margarine
1 (8-ounce) package cream cheese, softened
1 (14-ounce) can EAGLE BRAND® Sweetened Condensed Milk (NOT evaporated milk)
2 eggs
1 teaspoon vanilla extract
1½ cups (8-ounce package) English toffee bits, divided

1. Preheat oven to 350°F. In medium bowl, combine flour, powdered sugar, cocoa and baking soda; cut in butter until mixture is crumbly. Press firmly on bottom of ungreased 13×9-inch baking pan. Bake 15 minutes.

2. In large bowl, beat cream cheese until fluffy. Add EAGLE BRAND®, eggs and vanilla; beat until smooth. Stir in 1 cup English toffee bits. Pour mixture over hot crust. Bake 25 minutes or until set and edges just begin to brown.

3. Cool 15 minutes. Sprinkle remaining ½ cup English toffee bits evenly over top. Cool completely. Refrigerate several hours or until cold. Store leftovers covered in refrigerator.   *Makes about 3 dozen bars*

Prep Time: *20 minutes*
Bake Time: *40 minutes*
Cool Time: *15 minutes*

Cheesecakes

Triple Chocolate Cheesecakes

1. In 1-cup glass measure, combine gelatin and cold water; let stand 5 minutes to soften. Pour about 1 inch water into small saucepan; place glass measure in saucepan. Place saucepan over medium heat; stir until gelatin is dissolved. Remove measure from saucepan; cool slightly.

2. In large bowl, combine cream cheese, EAGLE BRAND® and melted chocolate; beat until smooth. Gradually beat in gelatin mixture. Fold in whipped topping and chocolate chips.

3. Spread pie filling on bottoms of crusts (optional). Spoon chocolate mixture into pie crusts. Cover and chill at least 4 hours. Store covered in refrigerator.

Makes 2 cheesecakes (12 servings total)

Prep Time: *20 minutes*
Chill Time: *4 hours*

Tip: To store these cheesecakes in the freezer, cover and freeze them for up to 1 month. Serve the cheesecakes frozen, or remove them from the freezer several hours before serving and let them thaw in the refrigerator.

1 envelope unflavored gelatin
½ cup cold water
2 (8-ounce) packages cream cheese, softened
1 (14-ounce) can EAGLE BRAND® Sweetened Condensed Milk (NOT evaporated milk)
4 (1-ounce) squares unsweetened chocolate, melted and slightly cooled
1 (8-ounce) carton frozen non-dairy whipped topping, thawed
½ cup miniature semisweet chocolate chips
1 (21-ounce) can cherry pie filling (optional)
2 (6-ounce) chocolate crumb crusts

Lemon Party Cheesecake

1 (18.25- or 18.5-ounce)
    package yellow cake
    mix*
4 eggs, divided
¼ cup vegetable oil*
2 (8-ounce) packages
    cream cheese, softened
1 (14-ounce) can EAGLE
    BRAND® Sweetened
    Condensed Milk
    (NOT evaporated milk)
¼ to ⅓ cup lemon juice
    from concentrate
2 teaspoons grated lemon
    peel (optional)
1 teaspoon vanilla extract

*If "pudding added" cake mix is used,
decrease oil to 3 tablespoons.

1. Preheat oven to 300°F. Reserve ½ cup dry cake mix. In large bowl, combine remaining cake mix, 1 egg and oil; mix well (mixture will be crumbly). Press firmly on bottom and 1½ inches up sides of greased 13×9-inch baking pan.

2. In same bowl, beat cream cheese until fluffy. Gradually beat in EAGLE BRAND® until smooth. Add remaining 3 eggs and reserved ½ cup cake mix; beat on medium speed of electric mixer 1 minute. Stir in lemon juice, lemon peel (optional) and vanilla. Pour into prepared crust.

3. Bake 50 to 55 minutes or until center is set. Cool to room temperature. Chill thoroughly. Cut into squares to serve. Garnish as desired. Store leftovers covered in refrigerator.   *Makes 1 dozen squares*

Prep Time: *20 minutes*
Bake Time: *50 to 55 minutes*

Frozen Mocha Cheesecake

1¼ cups chocolate wafer
    cookie crumbs (about
    24 wafers)
¼ cup sugar
¼ cup (½ stick) butter or
    margarine, melted
1 (8-ounce) package cream
    cheese, softened
1 (14-ounce) can EAGLE
    BRAND® Sweetened
    Condensed Milk
    (NOT evaporated milk)
⅔ cup chocolate-flavored
    syrup
1 to 2 tablespoons instant
    coffee
1 teaspoon hot water
1 cup (½ pint) whipping
    cream, whipped
    Additional chocolate
    crumbs (optional)

1. In medium bowl, combine cookie crumbs, sugar and butter; press firmly on bottom and up side of ungreased 8- or 9-inch springform pan or 13×9-inch baking pan.

2. In large bowl, beat cream cheese until fluffy. Gradually beat in EAGLE BRAND® and chocolate syrup until smooth.

3. In small bowl, dissolve coffee in water; add to cream cheese mixture. Mix well. Fold in whipped cream. Pour into prepared crust; cover. Freeze 6 hours or overnight. Garnish with chocolate crumbs (optional). Store leftovers covered in freezer.   *Makes one (8- or 9-inch) cheesecake*

Marbled Cheesecake Bars

1. Preheat oven to 300°F. Line 13×9-inch baking pan with foil; set aside. In medium bowl, combine cookie crumbs and butter; press firmly on bottom of prepared pan.

2. In large bowl, beat cream cheese until fluffy. Gradually beat in EAGLE BRAND® until smooth. Add eggs and vanilla; mix well. Pour half the batter evenly over prepared crust.

3. Stir melted chocolate into remaining batter; spoon over vanilla batter. With table knife or metal spatula, gently swirl through batter to marble.

4. Bake 45 to 50 minutes or until set. Cool. Chill. Cut into bars. Store covered in refrigerator. *Makes 2 to 3 dozen bars*

Prep Time: *20 minutes*
Bake Time: *45 to 50 minutes*

Tip: For even marbling, do not oversoften or overbeat the cream cheese.

2 cups finely crushed creme-filled chocolate sandwich cookie crumbs (about 24 cookies)

3 tablespoons butter or margarine, melted

3 (8-ounce) packages cream cheese, softened

1 (14-ounce) can EAGLE BRAND® Sweetened Condensed Milk (NOT evaporated milk)

3 eggs

2 teaspoons vanilla extract

2 (1-ounce) squares unsweetened chocolate, melted

Cheesecakes

German Chocolate Cheesecake Squares

1½ cups graham cracker crumbs
½ cup sugar
½ cup (1 stick) butter or margarine, melted
3 (8-ounce) packages cream cheese, softened
1 (14-ounce) can EAGLE BRAND® Sweetened Condensed Milk (NOT evaporated milk)
2 (4-ounce) packages semisweet chocolate, melted
3 eggs
1 tablespoon vanilla extract
Coconut Pecan Topping (recipe follows)

1. Preheat oven to 350°F. In medium bowl, combine graham cracker crumbs, sugar and butter; press firmly on bottom of ungreased 15×10×1-inch baking pan. In large bowl, beat cream cheese until fluffy. Gradually beat in EAGLE BRAND® until smooth. Add remaining ingredients except topping; mix well. Pour into prepared crust.

2. Bake 20 minutes or until center is set. Cool. Top with Coconut Pecan Topping. Chill. Store leftovers covered in refrigerator.

Makes 1 (15×10-inch) cheesecake

Coconut Pecan Topping

1 (14-ounce) can EAGLE BRAND® Sweetened Condensed Milk (NOT evaporated milk)
3 egg yolks
½ cup (1 stick) butter or margarine
1⅓ cups flaked coconut
1 cup chopped pecans
1 teaspoon vanilla extract

1. In heavy saucepan, combine EAGLE BRAND® and egg yolks; mix well. Add butter. Over medium-low heat, cook and stir until thickened and bubbly, 8 to 10 minutes.

2. Remove saucepan from heat; stir in coconut, pecans and vanilla. Cool 10 minutes.

Makes about 2¾ cups topping

Two-Tone Cheesecake Bars

1. Preheat oven to 300°F. In medium bowl, combine cookie crumbs and butter; press firmly on bottom of ungreased 13×9-inch baking pan.

2. In large bowl, beat cream cheese until fluffy. Gradually beat in EAGLE BRAND® until smooth. Add eggs and vanilla; mix well. Pour half the batter evenly into prepared crust. Stir melted chocolate into remaining batter; pour evenly over plain batter.

3. Bake 55 to 60 minutes or until set. Cool. Top with Chocolate Glaze. Chill. Cut into bars. Store leftovers covered in refrigerator.

Makes 2 to 3 dozen bars

Chocolate Glaze

   2 (1-ounce) squares unsweetened chocolate
   2 tablespoons butter or margarine
      Pinch salt
 1¾ cups sifted powdered sugar
   3 tablespoons hot water or cream

In heavy saucepan over low heat, melt chocolate and butter with salt. Remove from heat. Add powdered sugar and hot water or cream; mix well. Immediately spread over cheesecake.   *Makes about 1 cup glaze*

2 cups finely crushed creme-filled chocolate sandwich cookies (about 24 cookies)
3 tablespoons butter or margarine, melted
3 (8-ounce) packages cream cheese, softened
1 (14-ounce) can EAGLE BRAND® Sweetened Condensed Milk (NOT evaporated milk)
3 eggs
2 teaspoons vanilla extract
2 (1-ounce) squares unsweetened chocolate, melted
Chocolate Glaze (recipe follows)

Pies & Tarts

Banana Coconut Cream Pie

3 tablespoons cornstarch
1⅓ cups water
1 (14-ounce) can EAGLE
    BRAND® Sweetened
    Condensed Milk
    (NOT evaporated milk)
3 egg yolks, beaten
2 tablespoons butter
1 teaspoon vanilla extract
½ cup flaked coconut,
    toasted
2 medium bananas
2 tablespoons lemon juice
    from concentrate
1 (9-inch) pie crust, baked
    or 1 (6-ounce) graham
    cracker crumb crust
Whipped cream (optional)
Additional toasted
    coconut (optional)

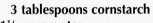

1. In heavy saucepan over medium heat, dissolve cornstarch in water; stir in EAGLE BRAND® and egg yolks. Cook and stir until thickened and bubbly. Remove from heat; add butter and vanilla. Cool slightly. Fold in coconut; set aside.

2. Peel and slice bananas into ¼-inch-thick rounds. Toss banana slices gently with lemon juice; drain. Arrange bananas on bottom of crust. Pour filling over bananas.

3. Cover; refrigerate 4 hours or until set. Top with whipped cream and toasted coconut (optional). Store leftovers covered in refrigerator.

Makes 1 (9-inch) pie

Chocolate-Topped Raspberry Cheese Pie

2 (3-ounce) packages cream cheese, softened
1 (14-ounce) can EAGLE BRAND® Sweetened Condensed Milk (NOT evaporated milk)
1 egg
3 tablespoons lemon juice from concentrate
1 teaspoon vanilla extract
1 cup fresh or frozen raspberries
1 (6-ounce) chocolate crumb crust
Chocolate Glaze (recipe follows)

1. Preheat oven to 350°F. In medium bowl, beat cream cheese until fluffy. Gradually beat in EAGLE BRAND® until smooth. Add egg, lemon juice and vanilla; mix well.

2. Arrange raspberries on bottom of crust. Slowly pour cheese mixture over fruit.

3. Bake 30 to 35 minutes or until center is almost set. Cool.

4. Prepare Chocolate Glaze and spread over cheesecake; chill. Garnish as desired. Store covered in refrigerator.   *Makes 1 pie*

Chocolate Glaze: In small saucepan over low heat, melt 2 (1-ounce) squares semisweet chocolate with ¼ cup whipping cream. Cook and stir until thickened and smooth. Remove from heat; cool slightly.

Prep Time: *15 minutes*
Bake Time: *30 to 35 minutes*

Apple Cranberry Streusel Custard Pie

1. Place rack in lower third of oven; preheat oven to 425°F. In large bowl, combine EAGLE BRAND® and cinnamon. Add eggs, water and fruits; mix well. Pour into crust.

2. In medium bowl, combine brown sugar and flour; cut in butter until crumbly. Add nuts. Sprinkle over pie. Bake 10 minutes.

3. Reduce oven temperature to 375°F; continue baking 30 to 40 minutes or until golden brown. Cool. Store covered in refrigerator.

Makes 1 (9-inch) pie

Prep Time: *25 minutes*
Bake Time: *40 to 50 minutes*

1 (14-ounce) can EAGLE BRAND® Sweetened Condensed Milk (NOT evaporated milk)
1 teaspoon ground cinnamon
2 eggs, beaten
½ cup hot water
1½ cups fresh or dry-pack frozen cranberries
2 medium all-purpose apples, peeled and sliced (about 1½ cups)
1 (9-inch) unbaked pie crust
½ cup firmly packed light brown sugar
½ cup all-purpose flour
¼ cup (½ stick) butter or margarine, softened
½ cup chopped nuts

Chocolate Pie

1 (14-ounce) can EAGLE BRAND® Sweetened Condensed Milk (NOT evaporated milk)

2 (1-ounce) squares unsweetened chocolate

¼ teaspoon salt

¼ cup hot water

½ teaspoon vanilla extract

1 cup whipping cream, whipped

1 baked pie crust, cooled

Additional whipped cream, shaved chocolate or chopped nuts (optional)

1. In top of double boiler, combine EAGLE BRAND®, chocolate and salt. Cook over hot water, stirring constantly, until mixture is very thick. Gradually add water, stir to keep mixture smooth. Continue to cook and stir 2 to 5 minutes, or until mixture thickens again. Remove from heat. Stir in vanilla.

2. Chill mixture in refrigerator or over ice water until cool. Fold whipped cream into cooled chocolate mixture. Pour into baked crust. Refrigerate 4 hours.

3. Garnish with additional whipped cream, shaved chocolate or chopped nuts (optional). Store leftovers covered in refrigerator.

Makes 1 (9-inch) pie

Cranberry Crumb Pie

1. Preheat oven to 425°F. Bake pie crust 6 minutes; remove from oven. Reduce oven temperature to 375°F.

2. In large bowl, beat cream cheese until fluffy. Gradually beat in EAGLE BRAND® until smooth. Stir in lemon juice. Pour into baked crust.

3. In small bowl, combine 1 tablespoon brown sugar and cornstarch; mix well. Stir in cranberry sauce. Spoon evenly over cheese mixture.

4. In medium bowl, combine flour and remaining 2 tablespoons brown sugar; cut in butter until crumbly. Stir in walnuts. Sprinkle evenly over cranberry mixture. Bake 45 to 50 minutes or until bubbly and golden. Cool. Serve at room temperature or chill thoroughly. Store leftovers covered in refrigerator.

Makes 1 (9-inch) pie

1 (9-inch) unbaked pie crust
1 (8-ounce) package cream cheese, softened
1 (14-ounce) can EAGLE BRAND® Sweetened Condensed Milk (NOT evaporated milk)
¼ cup lemon juice from concentrate
3 tablespoons light brown sugar, divided
2 tablespoons cornstarch
1 (16-ounce) can whole berry cranberry sauce
⅓ cup all-purpose flour
¼ cup (½ stick) cold butter or margarine
¾ cup chopped walnuts

Traditional Peanut Butter Pie

⅓ cup creamy peanut
   butter
½ cup powdered sugar
1 (9-inch) baked pie crust
1 (14-ounce) can EAGLE
   BRAND® Sweetened
   Condensed Milk
   (NOT evaporated milk)
4 eggs, separated
½ cup water
1 (4-serving size) package
   cook-and-serve vanilla
   pudding mix
1 (8-ounce) container sour
   cream, at room
   temperature
¼ teaspoon cream of tartar
6 tablespoons granulated
   sugar

1. Preheat oven to 350°F. In small bowl, cut peanut butter into powdered sugar until crumbly; sprinkle into baked crust.

2. In large saucepan, combine EAGLE BRAND®, egg yolks, water and pudding mix; cook and stir until thickened. Cool slightly; stir in sour cream. Spoon into pie crust.

3. In large bowl, beat egg whites and cream of tartar with electric mixer on high speed until soft peaks form. Gradually beat in sugar on medium speed, 1 tablespoon at a time; beat 4 minutes longer or until sugar is dissolved and stiff, glossy peaks form.

4. Spread meringue over pie, carefully sealing to edge of crust to prevent meringue from shrinking. Bake 15 minutes or until golden. Cool 1 hour. Chill at least 3 hours. Store leftovers covered in refrigerator.

Makes 1 (9-inch) pie

Apple Custard Tart

1. Let refrigerated pastry crust stand at room temperature according to package directions. Preheat oven to 375°F. On floured surface, roll pastry crust from center to edge, forming circle about 13 inches in diameter. Ease pastry into ungreased 11-inch tart pan with removable bottom. Trim pastry even with rim of pan. Place pan on baking sheet. Bake crust 15 minutes or until lightly golden.

2. Meanwhile, in medium bowl, beat EAGLE BRAND®, sour cream, apple juice concentrate, egg, vanilla and cinnamon until smooth. Pour into baked pie crust. Bake 25 minutes or until center appears set when shaken. Cool 1 hour on wire rack. Prepare Apple Cinnamon Glaze.

3. In large skillet, cook apples in butter until tender-crisp. Arrange apples on top of tart; drizzle with Apple Cinnamon Glaze. Chill in refrigerator at least 4 hours. Store leftovers loosely covered in refrigerator.

Makes 1 (11-inch) tart

Apple Cinnamon Glaze: In small saucepan over low heat, combine ⅓ cup thawed frozen apple juice concentrate, 1 teaspoon cornstarch and ½ teaspoon ground cinnamon. Mix well. Cook and stir until thick and bubbly.

Prep Time: *10 minutes*
Bake Time: *40 minutes*
Cool Time: *1 hour*
Chill Time: *4 hours*

1 folded refrigerated unbaked pastry crust (½ of 15-ounce package)
1 (14-ounce) can EAGLE BRAND® Sweetened Condensed Milk (NOT evaporated milk)
1½ cups sour cream
¼ cup thawed frozen apple juice concentrate
1 egg
1½ teaspoons vanilla extract
¼ teaspoon ground cinnamon
Apple Cinnamon Glaze (recipe follows)
2 medium all-purpose apples, cored, pared and thinly sliced
1 tablespoon butter

Creamy Lemon Pie

3 egg yolks
1 (14-ounce) can EAGLE
    BRAND® Sweetened
    Condensed Milk
    (NOT evaporated milk)
½ cup lemon juice from
    concentrate
1 (9-inch) baked pie crust
    or graham cracker
    crumb crust
Whipped topping or
    whipped cream
Freshly grated lemon
    peel (optional)

1. Preheat oven to 325°F. In medium bowl, beat egg yolks; gradually beat in EAGLE BRAND® and lemon juice. Pour into baked crust.

2. Bake 30 to 35 minutes or until set. Remove from oven. Cool 1 hour. Chill at least 3 hours.

3. Before serving, spread whipped topping or whipped cream over pie. Garnish with lemon peel (optional). Store leftovers covered in refrigerator.

Makes 1 (9-inch) pie

Deep-Dish Pumpkin Pie

1¾ cups all-purpose flour
⅓ cup granulated sugar
⅓ cup firmly packed light
    brown sugar
1 cup (2 sticks) cold butter
    or margarine, cut into
    small pieces
1 cup chopped nuts
1 (15-ounce) can pumpkin
    (2 cups)
1 (14-ounce) can EAGLE
    BRAND® Sweetened
    Condensed Milk
    (NOT evaporated milk)
2 eggs
1 teaspoon ground
    cinnamon
½ teaspoon ground allspice
½ teaspoon salt

1. Preheat oven to 350°F. In medium bowl, combine flour and sugars; cut in butter until crumbly. Stir in nuts. Reserve 1 cup crumb mixture; press remaining mixture firmly on bottom and halfway up sides of ungreased 12×7-inch baking pan.

2. In large bowl, combine remaining ingredients except reserved crumb mixture; mix well. Pour evenly into prepared crust. Top with reserved crumb mixture.

3. Bake 55 minutes or until golden. Cool. Serve with ice cream, if desired. Store leftovers covered in refrigerator.

Makes 1 (9-inch) pie

Chocolate Truffle Pie

1. In small saucepan, sprinkle gelatin over water; let stand 1 minute. Over low heat, stir until gelatin dissolves. Cool.

2. In large bowl, beat chocolate and EAGLE BRAND® with electric mixer on low speed until smooth. Stir in gelatin mixture and vanilla. Fold in whipped cream. Pour into crust.

3. Chill 3 hours or until set. Garnish as desired. Store leftovers covered in refrigerator.   *Makes 1 (9- or 10-inch) pie*

1 envelope unflavored gelatin
½ cup water
3 (1-ounce) squares unsweetened or semisweet chocolate, melted and cooled
1 (14-ounce) can EAGLE BRAND® Sweetened Condensed Milk (NOT evaporated milk)
1 teaspoon vanilla extract
2 cups (1 pint) whipping cream, whipped
1 (9- or 10-inch) chocolate crumb crust

Fudgy Pecan Pie

¼ cup (½ stick) butter or margarine
2 (1-ounce) squares unsweetened chocolate
1 (14-ounce) can EAGLE BRAND® Sweetened Condensed Milk (NOT evaporated milk)
½ cup hot water
2 eggs, well beaten
1¼ cups pecan halves or pieces
1 teaspoon vanilla extract
⅛ teaspoon salt
1 (9-inch) unbaked pie crust

1. Preheat oven to 350°F. In medium saucepan over low heat, melt butter and chocolate. Stir in EAGLE BRAND®, hot water and eggs; mix well. Remove from heat; stir in pecans, vanilla and salt. Pour into crust.

2. Bake 40 to 45 minutes or until center is set. Cool slightly. Serve warm or chilled. Garnish as desired. Store leftovers covered in refrigerator.

Makes 1 (9-inch) pie

Prep Time: *15 minutes*
Bake Time: *40 to 45 minutes*

Perfect Pumpkin Pie

1. Preheat oven to 425°F. In medium bowl, whisk pumpkin, EAGLE BRAND®, eggs, spices and salt until smooth. Pour into crust.

2. Bake 15 minutes. Reduce oven temperature to 350°F; bake 35 to 40 minutes longer. Cool. Garnish as desired. Store leftovers covered in refrigerator.

Makes 1 (9-inch) pie

Sour Cream Topping: In medium bowl, combine 1½ cups sour cream, 2 tablespoons sugar and 1 teaspoon vanilla extract. After pie has baked 30 minutes at 350°F, spread mixture evenly over top; bake 10 minutes.

Streusel Topping: In medium bowl, combine ½ cup packed brown sugar and ½ cup all-purpose flour; cut in ¼ cup (½ stick) cold butter or margarine until crumbly. Stir in ¼ cup chopped nuts. After pie has baked 30 minutes at 350°F, sprinkle streusel evenly over top; bake 10 minutes.

Chocolate Glaze: In small saucepan over low heat, melt ½ cup semisweet chocolate chips and 1 teaspoon solid shortening. Drizzle or spread over top of baked pie.

1 (15-ounce) can pumpkin (2 cups)
1 (14-ounce) can EAGLE BRAND® Sweetened Condensed Milk (NOT evaporated milk)
2 eggs
1 teaspoon ground cinnamon
½ teaspoon ground ginger
½ teaspoon ground nutmeg
½ teaspoon salt
1 (9-inch) unbaked pie crust

Lemon Icebox Pie

1 (14-ounce) can EAGLE BRAND® Sweetened Condensed Milk (NOT evaporated milk)
½ cup lemon juice from concentrate
Yellow food coloring (optional)
1 cup (½ pint) whipping cream, whipped
1 (9-inch) baked pie crust or graham cracker crumb crust

1. In medium bowl, combine EAGLE BRAND®, lemon juice and food coloring (optional); stir until well blended. Fold in whipped cream.

2. Pour into baked crust. Chill 3 hours or until set. Garnish as desired. Store leftovers covered in refrigerator.   *Makes 1 (9-inch) pie*

Pies & Tarts

Chocolate-Peanut Butter Mousse Pie

1. In medium bowl, combine graham cracker crumbs, peanuts and butter; press mixture on bottom and up side of ungreased 9-inch pie plate. Set aside.

2. Pour ½ cup whipping cream into microwave-safe bowl; microwave at HIGH (100% power) 2 minutes. Stir in ½ cup EAGLE BRAND® and chocolate chips until smooth. Spoon mixture into prepared crust. Chill 1 hour.

3. In large bowl, beat remaining 1 cup whipping cream until stiff peaks form; set aside. In small bowl, beat remaining EAGLE BRAND®, cream cheese and peanut butter until smooth. Fold in ⅓ of whipped cream; fold in remaining whipped cream. Spoon over chocolate filling. Chill 1 hour. Garnish as desired. Store leftovers covered in refrigerator.   *Make 1 (9-inch) pie*

Prep Time: *20 minutes*
Chill Time: *2 hours*

1 cup chocolate graham cracker crumbs
⅓ cup honey-roasted peanuts, finely chopped
6 tablespoons butter or margarine, softened
1½ cups whipping cream, divided
1 (14-ounce) can EAGLE BRAND® Sweetened Condensed Milk (NOT evaporated milk), divided
1½ cups semisweet chocolate chips
2 (3-ounce) packages cream cheese, softened
¾ cup creamy peanut butter

Chocolate Chiffon Pie

2 (1-ounce) squares unsweetened chocolate, chopped
1 (14-ounce) can EAGLE BRAND® Sweetened Condensed Milk (NOT evaporated milk)
1 envelope unflavored gelatin
⅓ cup water
½ teaspoon vanilla extract
1 cup (½ pint) whipping cream, whipped
1 (6-ounce) chocolate or graham cracker crumb crust
Additional whipped cream and shaved chocolate

1. In heavy saucepan over low heat, melt chocolate with EAGLE BRAND®. Remove from heat.

2. Meanwhile, in small saucepan, sprinkle gelatin over water; let stand 1 minute. Over low heat, stir until gelatin dissolves.

3. Stir gelatin into chocolate mixture. Add vanilla. Cool to room temperature. Fold in whipped cream. Spread into crust.

4. Chill 3 hours or until set. Garnish with additional whipped cream and shaved chocolate. Store leftovers covered in refrigerator.   *Makes 1 pie*

Prep Time: *20 minutes*
Chill Time: *3 hours*

Pies & Tarts

Peanut Butter Pie

1. Prepare Chocolate Crunch Crust.

2. In large bowl, beat cream cheese until fluffy. Gradually beat in EAGLE BRAND® and peanut butter until smooth. Stir in lemon juice and vanilla. Fold in whipped cream.

3. Spread EAGLE BRAND® mixture in prepared crust. Drizzle topping over pie. Refrigerate 4 to 5 hours or until firm. Store leftovers covered in refrigerator. *Makes 1 (9-inch) pie*

Chocolate Crunch Crust: In heavy saucepan over low heat, melt ⅓ cup butter or margarine and 1 (6-ounce) package semisweet chocolate chips. Remove from heat; gently stir in 2½ cups oven-toasted rice cereal until completely coated. Press on bottom and up side to rim of buttered 9-inch pie plate. Chill 30 minutes.

Chocolate Crunch Crust (recipe follows)
1 (8-ounce) package cream cheese, softened
1 (14-ounce) can EAGLE BRAND® Sweetened Condensed Milk (NOT evaporated milk)
¾ cup creamy peanut butter
2 tablespoons lemon juice from concentrate
1 teaspoon vanilla extract
1 cup whipping cream, whipped *or* 1 (4-ounce) container frozen non-dairy whipped topping, thawed
Chocolate fudge ice cream topping

Microwave Caramel Nut Cream Pie

1 (14-ounce) can EAGLE
   BRAND® Sweetened
   Condensed Milk
   (NOT evaporated milk)
1 cup chopped nuts
2 tablespoons milk
½ teaspoon ground
   cinnamon
1 cup (½ pint) whipping
   cream, whipped
1 (6-ounce) graham
   cracker crumb crust

1. Pour EAGLE BRAND® into microwave-safe 2-quart glass measure; microwave at MEDIUM (50% power) 4 minutes, stirring briskly every 2 minutes until smooth. Microwave at LOW (30% power) 12 to 18 minutes or until very thick and caramel-colored, stirring briskly every 2 minutes until smooth.

2. Stir nuts, milk and cinnamon into warm caramelized milk; cool to room temperature. Fold in whipped cream. Pour into crust.

3. Chill 3 hours or until set. Garnish as desired. Refrigerate leftovers.

Makes 1 (9-inch) pie

Prep Time: *25 minutes*
Microwave Time: *16 to 22 minutes*
Chill Time: *3 hours*

Streusel Topped Pumpkin Pie

1 (15-ounce) can pumpkin
   (2 cups)
1 (14-ounce) can EAGLE
   BRAND® Sweetened
   Condensed Milk
   (NOT evaporated milk)
1 egg
1¼ teaspoons ground
   cinnamon, divided
½ teaspoon salt
½ teaspoon ground ginger
½ teaspoon ground nutmeg
1 (8- or 9-inch) prepared
   graham cracker crust
¼ cup firmly packed light
   brown sugar
2 tablespoons all-purpose
   flour
2 tablespoons cold butter
¾ cup chopped walnuts

1. Preheat oven to 425°F. In medium bowl, whisk pumpkin, EAGLE BRAND®, egg, ¾ teaspoon cinnamon, salt, ginger and nutmeg. Pour into crust. Bake 15 minutes.

2. In small bowl, combine brown sugar, flour and remaining ½ teaspoon cinnamon; cut in butter until crumbly. Stir in walnuts. Remove pie from oven; reduce oven temperature to 350°F. Sprinkle streusel mixture over pie.

3. Bake 40 minutes or until set. Cool. Serve warm or at room temperature. Store leftovers covered in refrigerator. *Makes 1 (8- or 9-inch) pie*

Prep Time: *30 minutes*
Bake Time: *55 minutes*

Tip: Top with whipped cream just before serving, if desired.

Key Lime Pie

1. Preheat oven to 325°F. In medium bowl, beat egg yolks; gradually beat in EAGLE BRAND® and lime juice. Stir in food coloring (optional). Pour into crust.

2. Bake 30 minutes. Remove from oven. Increase oven temperature to 350°F.

3. Meanwhile for meringue, in another medium bowl with clean mixer, beat egg whites and cream of tartar until soft peaks form. Gradually beat in sugar, 1 tablespoon at a time. Beat 4 minutes or until stiff, glossy peaks form and sugar is dissolved.

4. Immediately spread meringue over hot pie, carefully sealing to edge of crust to prevent shrinking. Bake 15 minutes. Cool 1 hour. Chill at least 3 hours. Store leftovers covered in refrigerator.   *Makes 1 (9-inch) pie*

Prep Time: *25 minutes*
Bake Time: *45 minutes*
Cool Time: *1 hour*
Chill Time: *3 hours*

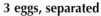

3 eggs, separated
1 (14-ounce) can EAGLE BRAND® Sweetened Condensed Milk (NOT evaporated milk)
½ cup key lime juice from concentrate
2 to 3 drops green food coloring (optional)
1 (9-inch) unbaked pie crust
½ teaspoon cream of tartar
⅓ cup sugar

Pies & Tarts

Cherry-Topped Lemon Cheesecake Pie

1 (8-ounce) package cream cheese, softened

1 (14-ounce) can EAGLE BRAND® Sweetened Condensed Milk (NOT evaporated milk)

⅓ cup lemon juice from concentrate

1 teaspoon vanilla extract

1 (6-ounce) graham cracker crumb crust

1 (21-ounce) can cherry pie filling, chilled

1. In large bowl, beat cream cheese until fluffy. Gradually beat in EAGLE BRAND® until smooth. Stir in lemon juice and vanilla. Pour into crust.

2. Chill at least 3 hours. To serve, top with cherry pie filling. Store leftovers covered in refrigerator. *Makes 6 to 8 servings*

Prep Time: *10 minutes*
Chill Time: *3 hours*

Note: For a firmer crust, brush crust with beaten egg white; bake in preheated 375°F oven 5 minutes. Cool before pouring filling into crust.

Pies & Tarts

Sweet Potato Pecan Pie

1. Preheat oven to 425°F. In large bowl, beat hot sweet potatoes and butter until smooth. Add EAGLE BRAND® and remaining ingredients except crust and Pecan Topping; mix well. Pour into crust.

2. Bake 20 minutes. Meanwhile, prepare Pecan Topping.

3. Remove pie from oven; reduce oven temperature to 350°F. Spoon Pecan Topping over pie.

4. Bake 25 minutes longer or until set. Cool. Serve warm or at room temperature. Store leftovers covered in refrigerator.

Makes 1 (8- or 9-inch) pie

Pecan Topping: In small bowl, beat 1 egg, 2 tablespoons firmly packed light brown sugar, 2 tablespoons dark corn syrup, 1 tablespoon melted butter and ½ teaspoon maple flavoring. Stir in 1 cup chopped pecans.

Prep Time: *30 minutes*
Bake Time: *45 minutes*

1 pound sweet potatoes, cooked and peeled
¼ cup (½ stick) butter or margarine, softened
1 (14-ounce) can EAGLE BRAND® Sweetened Condensed Milk (NOT evaporated milk)
1 egg
1 teaspoon freshly grated orange peel
1 teaspoon ground cinnamon
1 teaspoon vanilla extract
½ teaspoon ground nutmeg
¼ teaspoon salt
1 (8- or 9-inch) prepared graham cracker crust
Pecan Topping (recipe follows)

Decadent Brownie Pie

1 (9-inch) unbaked pie
    crust
1 cup (6 ounces) semisweet
    chocolate chips
¼ cup (½ stick) butter or
    margarine
1 (14-ounce) can EAGLE
    BRAND® Sweetened
    Condensed Milk
    (NOT evaporated milk)
½ cup biscuit baking mix
2 eggs
1 teaspoon vanilla extract
1 cup chopped nuts
    Vanilla ice cream

1. Preheat oven to 375°F. Bake pie crust 10 minutes; remove from oven. Reduce oven temperature to 325°F.

2. In small saucepan over low heat, melt chocolate chips with butter.

3. In large bowl, beat chocolate mixture, EAGLE BRAND®, biscuit mix, eggs and vanilla until smooth. Add nuts. Pour into baked crust.

4. Bake 35 to 40 minutes or until center is set. Serve warm or at room temperature with ice cream. Store leftovers covered in refrigerator.

Makes 1 (9-inch) pie

Prep Time: *25 minutes*
Bake Time: *45 to 50 minutes*

Pies & Tarts

Holiday Cheese Tarts

1. In large bowl, beat cream cheese until fluffy. Gradually beat in EAGLE BRAND® until smooth. Stir in lemon juice and vanilla. Spoon into crusts.

2. Chill 2 hours or until set. Just before serving, top with fruit; brush with jelly (optional). Store leftovers covered in refrigerator.

Makes 1 dozen tarts

Prep Time: *10 minutes*
Chill Time: *2 hours*

1 (8-ounce) package cream cheese, softened
1 (14-ounce) can EAGLE BRAND® Sweetened Condensed Milk (NOT evaporated milk)
⅓ cup lemon juice from concentrate
1 teaspoon vanilla extract
2 (4-ounce) packages single-serve graham cracker crumb crusts
Assorted fruit (cherries, blueberries, raspberries, strawberries, orange segments, kiwi fruit, grapes, etc.)
¼ cup apple jelly, melted (optional)

Creamy Lemon Meringue Pie

3 eggs, separated
1 (14-ounce) can EAGLE
   BRAND® Sweetened
   Condensed Milk
   (NOT evaporated milk)
½ cup lemon juice from
   concentrate
2 to 3 drops yellow food
   coloring (optional)
1 (8- or 9-inch) baked pie
   crust or graham
   cracker crumb crust
¼ teaspoon cream of tartar
⅓ cup sugar

1. Preheat oven to 350°F. In medium bowl, beat egg yolks; stir in EAGLE BRAND®, lemon juice and food coloring (optional). Pour into baked crust.

2. In large bowl, beat egg whites and cream of tartar until soft peaks form. Gradually beat in sugar, 1 tablespoon at at time; beat 4 minutes longer or until sugar is dissolved and stiff glossy peaks form. Spread meringue over pie, sealing carefully to edge of crust.

3. Bake 12 to 15 minutes or until meringue is lightly brown. Cool. Chill thoroughly. Store leftovers covered in refrigerator.

Makes one (8- or 9-inch) pie

Pecan Pie Bars

2 cups all-purpose flour
½ cup powdered sugar
1 cup (2 sticks) cold butter
   or margarine
1 (14-ounce) can EAGLE
   BRAND® Sweetened
   Condensed Milk
   (NOT evaporated milk)
1 egg
1 teaspoon vanilla extract
1 (6-ounce) package
   chocolate-covered
   toffee bits or almond
   brickle chips
1 cup chopped pecans

1. Preheat oven to 350°F (325°F for glass dish). In medium bowl, combine flour and powdered sugar; cut in butter until crumbly. Press firmly on bottom of ungreased 13×9-inch baking pan. Bake 15 minutes.

2. Meanwhile, in medium bowl, beat EAGLE BRAND®, egg and vanilla. Stir in toffee bits and pecans. Spread evenly over baked crust.

3. Bake 25 minutes or until golden brown. Cool. Chill thoroughly. Cut into bars. Store leftovers covered in refrigerator.

Makes 3 dozen bars

Heavenly Chocolate Mousse Pie

1. In medium bowl, beat EAGLE BRAND®, melted chocolate and vanilla until well blended.

2. Chill 15 minutes or until cooled; stir until smooth. Fold in whipped cream.

3. Pour into crust. Chill thoroughly. Garnish as desired. Store leftovers covered in refrigerator.

Makes 1 (9-inch) pie

Prep Time: *20 minutes*

1 (14-ounce) can EAGLE BRAND® Sweetened Condensed Milk (NOT evaporated milk)

4 (1-ounce) squares unsweetened chocolate, melted

1½ teaspoons vanilla extract

1 cup (½ pint) whipping cream, whipped

1 (6-ounce) chocolate crumb crust

Desserts

Peach Cream Cake

1 (10¾-ounce) loaf angel
   food cake, frozen
1 (14-ounce) can EAGLE
   BRAND® Sweetened
   Condensed Milk
   (NOT evaporated milk)
1 cup cold water
1 teaspoon almond extract
1 (4-serving-size) package
   instant vanilla pudding
   and pie filling mix
2 cups (1 pint) whipping
   cream, whipped
4 cups sliced peeled fresh
   peaches (about
   2 pounds)

1. Cut cake into ¼-inch slices; arrange half the slices on bottom of ungreased 13×9-inch baking dish.

2. In large bowl, combine EAGLE BRAND®, water and almond extract. Add pudding mix; beat well. Chill 5 minutes.

3. Fold in whipped cream. Spread half the pudding mixture over cake slices; arrange half the peach slices on top. Repeat layering, ending with peach slices. Chill 4 hours or until set. Cut into squares to serve. Store leftovers covered in refrigerator.

Makes 1 (13×9-inch) cake

Double Chocolate Ice Cream Squares

1½ cups finely crushed
   creme-filled chocolate
   sandwich cookies
   (about 18 cookies)
2 to 3 tablespoons butter
   or margarine, melted
1 (14-ounce) can EAGLE
   BRAND® Sweetened
   Condensed Milk
   (NOT evaporated milk)
3 (1-ounce) squares
   unsweetened
   chocolate, melted
2 teaspoons vanilla extract
1 cup chopped nuts
   (optional)
2 cups (1 pint) whipping
   cream, whipped
   Whipped topping

1. In medium bowl, combine cookie crumbs and butter; press firmly on bottom of ungreased 13×9-inch baking pan.

2. In large bowl, beat EAGLE BRAND®, melted chocolate and vanilla until well blended. Stir in nuts (optional). Fold in whipped cream. Pour into prepared crust. Spread with whipped topping. Cover; freeze 6 hours or until firm. Garnish with additional finely chopped nuts or as desired. Store leftovers covered in freezer. *Makes about 1 dozen squares*

Rocky Road Ice Cream Squares: Substitute chopped peanuts for nuts; add 1 cup miniature marshmallows to EAGLE BRAND® mixture. Proceed as directed above.

Cherry-Berry Crumble

1. In medium saucepan over medium heat, cook and stir cherry pie filling and raspberries until heated through. Stir in EAGLE BRAND®; cook and stir 1 minute.

2. Spoon into ungreased 2-quart square baking dish or 6 individual dessert dishes. Sprinkle with granola; garnish as desired. Serve warm. Store leftovers covered in refrigerator. *Makes 6 servings*

Prep Time: *10 minutes*

Peach-Berry Crumble: Substitute peach pie filling for cherry pie filling.

Cherry-Rhubarb Crumble: Substitute fresh or frozen sliced rhubarb for raspberries. In medium saucepan over medium-high heat, cook and stir pie filling and rhubarb until bubbly. Cook and stir 5 minutes more. Proceed as directed above.

1 (21-ounce) can cherry pie filling
2 cups fresh or frozen raspberries
1 (14-ounce) can EAGLE BRAND® Sweetened Condensed Milk (NOT evaporated milk)
1½ cups granola

Desserts

Creamy Rice Pudding

1½ cups water
½ cup long grain rice*
1 cinnamon stick
1 (1-inch) piece orange or
  lemon peel
1 (14-ounce) can EAGLE
  BRAND® Sweetened
  Condensed Milk
  (NOT evaporated milk)
Dash salt
½ cup raisins or pecan
  halves (optional)

*DO NOT use quick cooking rice.

1. In medium saucepan, combine water, rice, cinnamon stick, orange peel and salt. Bring to a boil; reduce heat. Cover and simmer 15 minutes.

2. Stir in EAGLE BRAND®. Cook uncovered over low heat, stirring frequently 25 minutes or until rice is tender. Remove cinnamon stick and orange peel. Cool. (Pudding will thicken as it cools.) Stir in raisins or nuts (optional). Serve warm or chilled. *Makes 4 (½-cup) servings*

Prep Time: 5 minutes
Cook Time: 40 minutes

German Chocolate Cake

1. Preheat oven to 350°F. Grease and flour 13×9-inch baking pan. In large bowl, combine cake mix, water, 3 eggs, oil and ⅓ cup EAGLE BRAND®. Beat at low speed of electric mixer until moistened; beat at high speed 2 minutes.

2. Pour into prepared pan. Bake 40 to 45 minutes or until wooden pick inserted near center comes out clean.

3. In small saucepan over medium heat, combine remaining EAGLE BRAND®, butter and egg yolk. Cook and stir until thickened, about 6 minutes. Add pecans, coconut and vanilla; spread over warm cake. Store leftovers covered in refrigerator.   *Makes 10 to 12 servings*

Prep Time: 15 minutes
Bake Time: 40 to 45 minutes

1 (18.25-ounce) package chocolate cake mix
1 cup water
3 eggs
½ cup vegetable oil
1 (14-ounce) can EAGLE BRAND® Sweetened Condensed Milk (NOT evaporated milk), divided
3 tablespoons butter or margarine
1 egg yolk
⅓ cup chopped pecans
⅓ cup flaked coconut
1 teaspoon vanilla extract

Raspberry Almond Trifles

2 cups whipping cream
¼ cup plus 1 tablespoon
  raspberry liqueur or
  orange juice, divided
1 (14-ounce) can EAGLE
  BRAND® Sweetened
  Condensed Milk
  (NOT evaporated milk)
2 (3-ounce) packages
  ladyfingers, separated
1 cup seedless raspberry
  jam
½ cup sliced almonds,
  toasted

1. In large bowl, beat whipping cream and 1 tablespoon liqueur until stiff peaks form. Fold in EAGLE BRAND®; set aside.

2. Layer bottom of 12 ungreased (4-ounce) custard cups or ramekins with ladyfingers. Brush with some remaining liqueur. Spread half of jam over ladyfingers. Spread evenly with half of cream mixture; sprinkle with half of almonds. Repeat layers with remaining ladyfingers, liqueur, jam, cream mixture and almonds. Cover and chill 2 hours. Store covered in refrigerator.

Makes 12 servings

Prep Time: *20 minutes*
Chill Time: *2 hours*

Desserts

Fudgy Milk Chocolate Fondue

1. In heavy saucepan over medium heat, combine syrup, EAGLE BRAND® and salt. Cook and stir 12 to 15 minutes or until slightly thickened.

2. Remove from heat; stir in vanilla. Serve warm with assorted dippers. Store leftovers covered in refrigerator.   *Makes about 3 cups fondue*

Prep Time: *12 to 15 minutes*

Microwave Directions: In 1-quart glass measure, combine syrup, EAGLE BRAND® and salt. Microwave at HIGH (100% power) 3½ to 4 minutes, stirring after 2 minutes. Stir in vanilla.

Tip: Can be served warm or cold over ice cream. Can be made several weeks ahead. Store tightly covered in refrigerator.

1 (16-ounce) can chocolate-flavored syrup
1 (14-ounce) can EAGLE BRAND® Sweetened Condensed Milk (NOT evaporated milk)
Dash salt
1½ teaspoons vanilla extract
Assorted dippers: cookies, cake cubes, pound cake cubes, angel food cake cubes, banana chunks, apple slices, strawberries, pear slices, kiwifruit slices and/or marshmallows

Desserts

Baked Almond Pudding

¼ cup firmly packed light
    brown sugar
¾ cup slivered almonds,
    toasted
1 (14-ounce) can EAGLE
    BRAND® Sweetened
    Condensed Milk
    (NOT evaporated milk)
5 eggs
1 cup whipping cream,
    divided
½ teaspoon almond extract
    Additional toasted
    almonds (optional)

1. Preheat oven to 350°F. In ungreased 8-inch round cake pan, sprinkle brown sugar; set aside. In blender or food processor container, grind almonds; add EAGLE BRAND®, eggs, ½ cup whipping cream and almond extract. Blend thoroughly. Pour into prepared pan; set in larger pan. Fill larger pan with 1 inch hot water.

2. Bake 40 to 45 minutes or until knife inserted near center comes out clean. Cool. Chill thoroughly; invert onto serving plate. In medium bowl, beat remaining ½ cup whipping cream for garnish; top with additional almonds (optional). Store leftovers covered in refrigerator.   *Makes 8 to 10 servings*

Chocolate Sheet Cake

1¼ cups (2½ sticks) butter or
    margarine, divided
1 cup water
½ cup unsweetened cocoa,
    divided
2 cups all-purpose flour
1½ cups firmly packed light
    brown sugar
1 teaspoon baking soda
1 teaspoon ground
    cinnamon
½ teaspoon salt
1 (14-ounce) can EAGLE
    BRAND® Sweetened
    Condensed Milk
    (NOT evaporated
    milk), divided
2 eggs
1 teaspoon vanilla extract
1 cup powdered sugar
1 cup chopped nuts

1. Preheat oven to 350°F. In small saucepan over medium heat, melt 1 cup butter; stir in water and ¼ cup cocoa. Bring to a boil; remove from heat. In large bowl, combine flour, brown sugar, baking soda, cinnamon and salt. Add cocoa mixture; beat well. Stir in ⅓ cup EAGLE BRAND®, eggs and vanilla. Pour into greased 15×10×1-inch baking pan. Bake 15 minutes or until cake springs back when lightly touched.

2. In small saucepan over medium heat, melt remaining ¼ cup butter; add remaining ¼ cup cocoa and remaining EAGLE BRAND®. Stir in powdered sugar and nuts. Spread over warm cake.   *Makes 1 (15×10-inch) cake*

Chocolate Almond Torte

1. Line 2 (8- or 9-inch) round cake pans with wax paper. Preheat oven to 350°F. In small bowl, beat egg whites until soft peaks form; set aside.

2. In large bowl, beat butter and sugar until fluffy. Add egg yolks and extracts; mix well.

3. In medium bowl, combine almonds, flour, cocoa, baking powder and baking soda; add alternately with milk to butter mixture, beating well after each addition.

4. Fold in beaten egg whites. Pour into prepared pans. Bake 18 to 20 minutes or until wooden picks inserted near centers come out clean. Cool 10 minutes; remove from pans. Cool completely.

5. Prepare Chocolate Almond Frosting. Split each cake layer; fill and frost with frosting. Garnish as desired. Store covered in refrigerator.

Makes 1 (8- or 9-inch) layer cake

Prep Time: *30 minutes*
Bake Time: *18 to 20 minutes*

Chocolate Almond Frosting

2 (1-ounce) squares semisweet chocolate, chopped
**1 (14-ounce) can EAGLE BRAND® Sweetened Condensed Milk
    (NOT evaporated milk)**
1 teaspoon almond extract

1. In heavy saucepan over medium heat, melt chocolate with EAGLE BRAND®. Cook and stir until mixture thickens, about 10 minutes.

2. Remove from heat; cool 10 minutes. Stir in almond extract; cool.

Makes about 1½ cups frosting

Prep Time: *20 minutes*

4 eggs, separated
**½ cup (1 stick) butter or
    margarine, softened**
1 cup sugar
1 teaspoon almond extract
1 teaspoon vanilla extract
**1 cup finely chopped
    toasted almonds**
¾ cup all-purpose flour
½ cup unsweetened cocoa
½ teaspoon baking powder
½ teaspoon baking soda
⅔ cup milk
**Chocolate Almond
    Frosting (recipe
    follows)**

2 tablespoons instant coffee crystals
½ cup hot water
2 (3-ounce) packages ladyfingers (24), cut crosswise into quarters
1 (14-ounce) can EAGLE BRAND® Sweetened Condensed Milk (NOT evaporated milk), divided
8 ounces mascarpone or cream cheese, softened
2 cups (1 pint) whipping cream, divided
1 teaspoon vanilla extract
1 cup (6 ounces) miniature semisweet chocolate chips, divided

Tiramisu

1. In small bowl, dissolve coffee crystals in water; reserve 1 tablespoon coffee mixture. Brush remaining coffee mixture on cut sides of ladyfingers; set aside.

2. In large bowl, beat ¾ cup EAGLE BRAND® and mascarpone. Add 1¼ cups cream, vanilla and reserved 1 tablespoon coffee mixture; beat until soft peaks form. Fold in ½ cup chocolate chips.

3. In heavy saucepan over low heat, melt remaining ½ cup chocolate chips with remaining EAGLE BRAND®.

4. Using 8 tall dessert glasses or parfait glasses, layer mascarpone mixture, chocolate mixture and ladyfinger pieces, beginning and ending with mascarpone mixture. Cover and chill at least 4 hours.

5. In medium bowl, beat remaining ¾ cup cream until soft peaks form. To serve, spoon whipped cream over dessert. Garnish as desired. Store leftovers covered in refrigerator. *Makes 8 servings*

Desserts

Frozen Lemon Squares

1. Preheat oven to 325°F. In small bowl, combine graham cracker crumbs, sugar and butter; press firmly on bottom of ungreased 8- or 9-inch square pan.

2. In small bowl, beat EAGLE BRAND®, egg yolks, lemon juice and food coloring (optional). Pour into prepared crust.

3. Bake 30 minutes. Cool completely. Top with whipped cream. Freeze 4 hours or until firm. Let stand 10 minutes before serving. Garnish as desired. Store leftovers covered in freezer.   *Makes 6 to 9 servings*

1¼ **cups graham cracker crumbs**
¼ **cup sugar**
¼ **cup (½ stick) butter or margarine, melted**
1 **(14-ounce) can EAGLE BRAND® Sweetened Condensed Milk (NOT evaporated milk)**
3 **egg yolks**
½ **cup lemon juice from concentrate**
  Yellow food coloring (optional)
  Whipped cream or non-dairy whipped topping

Strawberries & Cream Dessert

1 (14-ounce) can EAGLE
   BRAND® Sweetened
   Condensed Milk
   (NOT evaporated milk)
1½ cups cold water
1 (4-serving-size) package
   instant vanilla pudding
   and pie filling mix
2 cups (1 pint) whipping
   cream, whipped
1 (12-ounce) prepared loaf
   pound cake, cut into
   cubes (about 6 cups)
4 cups sliced fresh
   strawberries
½ cup strawberry preserves
   Additional sliced fresh
   strawberries
   Toasted slivered almonds

1. In large bowl, combine EAGLE BRAND® and water; mix well. Add pudding mix; beat until well blended. Chill 5 minutes. Fold in whipped cream.

2. Spoon 2 cups pudding mixture into 4-quart round glass serving bowl; top with half the cake cubes, half the strawberries, half the preserves and half the remaining pudding mixture. Repeat layers of cake cubes, strawberries and preserves; top with remaining pudding mixture. Garnish with additional strawberries and almonds. Chill 4 hours or until set. Store covered in refrigerator.   *Makes 10 to 12 servings*

Variation: Here is another way to layer this spectacular dessert: Spoon 2 cups pudding mixture into 4-quart round glass serving bowl; top with the cake cubes, all of the strawberries, all of the preserves and the remaining pudding mixture. Garnish and chill as directed above.

Chocolate Peanut Butter Dessert Sauce

1. In medium saucepan over medium-low heat, melt chocolate and peanut butter with EAGLE BRAND® and milk, stirring constantly.

2. Remove from heat; stir in vanilla. Cool slightly. Serve warm over ice cream, cake or as fruit dipping sauce. Store covered in refrigerator.

Makes about 1½ cups sauce

Prep Time: *15 minutes*

2 (1-ounce) squares semisweet chocolate, chopped
2 tablespoons creamy peanut butter
1 (14-ounce) can EAGLE BRAND® Sweetened Condensed Milk (NOT evaporated milk)
2 tablespoons milk
1 teaspoon vanilla extract

Golden Bread Pudding

4 cups soft white bread cubes (5 slices)
3 eggs
1 teaspoon ground cinnamon
3 cups warm water
1 (14-ounce) can EAGLE BRAND® Sweetened Condensed Milk (NOT evaporated milk)
2 tablespoons butter or margarine, melted
2 teaspoons vanilla extract
½ teaspoon salt
Butter Rum Sauce (recipe follows)

1. Preheat oven to 350°F. Place bread cubes in buttered 9-inch square baking pan. In large bowl, beat eggs and cinnamon; add remaining ingredients except Butter Rum Sauce. Pour evenly over bread cubes, moistening completely.

2. Bake 45 to 50 minutes or until knife inserted in center comes out clean. Cool. Serve warm with Butter Rum Sauce. Store leftovers covered in refrigerator. *Makes 6 to 9 servings*

Butter Rum Sauce: In medium saucepan over medium-high heat, melt ¼ cup (½ stick) butter or margarine; add ¾ cup firmly packed light brown sugar and ½ cup whipping cream. Boil rapidly 8 to 10 minutes; add 2 tablespoons rum or 1 teaspoon rum flavoring. Serve warm. Makes about 1 cup sauce.

Desserts

Ambrosia Freeze

1. In large bowl with electric mixer on low speed, beat cream cheese and bananas until nearly smooth. Beat in EAGLE BRAND®, yogurt and lemon juice. Stir in orange sections, pineapple and coconut. Stir in food coloring (optional). Spoon into ungreased 11×7-inch baking dish. Cover and freeze 6 hours or until firm.

2. Remove from freezer 15 minutes before serving. Cut into 1×1-inch cubes; serve in stemmed glasses or dessert dishes.   *Makes 8 to 10 servings*

1 (8-ounce) container strawberry cream cheese
2 medium bananas
1 (14-ounce) can EAGLE BRAND® Sweetened Condensed Milk (NOT evaporated milk)
1 (8-ounce) container low-fat strawberry yogurt
2 tablespoons lemon juice from concentrate
1 (11-ounce) can mandarin orange sections, drained
1 (8-ounce) can crushed pineapple, well drained
½ cup toasted flaked coconut
Red food coloring (optional)

Chocolate-Caramel Fondue

3 (1-ounce) squares
  unsweetened
  chocolate, chopped
1 (14-ounce) can EAGLE
  BRAND® Sweetened
  Condensed Milk
  (NOT evaporated milk)
1 (12¼-ounce) jar caramel
  ice cream topping
  Dippers: Fresh fruit,
  cookies, pound cake
  pieces or angel food
  cake pieces

1. In medium saucepan, melt chocolate with EAGLE BRAND® and caramel topping.

2. Pour into serving bowl or individual cups. Serve with desired dippers.

Makes 2½ cups fondue

Prep Time : *15 minutes*

Quick Chocolate Mousse

1 (14-ounce) can EAGLE
  BRAND® Sweetened
  Condensed Milk
  (NOT evaporated milk)
1 (4-serving-size) package
  instant chocolate
  pudding and pie filling
  mix
1 cup cold water
1 cup (½ pint) whipping
  cream, whipped

1. In large bowl, beat EAGLE BRAND®, pudding mix and water; chill 5 minutes.

2. Fold in whipped cream. Spoon into serving dishes; chill. Garnish as desired.

Makes 8 to 10 servings

Prep Time: *5 minutes*

Desserts

Blueberry Streusel Cobbler

1. Preheat oven to 325°F. In medium bowl, combine blueberries, EAGLE BRAND® and lemon peel.

2. In large bowl, cut ¾ cup butter into 1½ cups biscuit mix until crumbly; add blueberry mixture. Spread in greased 9-inch square baking pan.

3. In small bowl, combine remaining ½ cup biscuit mix and brown sugar; cut in remaining 2 tablespoons butter until crumbly. Add nuts. Sprinkle over cobbler.

4. Bake 1 hour and 10 minutes or until golden. Serve warm with vanilla ice cream and Blueberry Sauce. Store leftovers covered in refrigerator.

Makes 8 to 12 servings

Blueberry Sauce: In large saucepan over medium heat, combine ½ cup sugar, 1 tablespoon cornstarch, ½ teaspoon ground cinnamon and ¼ teaspoon ground nutmeg. Gradually add ½ cup water. Cook and stir until thickened. Stir in 1 pint blueberries; cook and stir until hot. Makes about 1⅔ cups sauce.

Prep Time: *15 minutes*
Bake Time: *1 hour and 10 minutes*

---

1 pint fresh or frozen blueberries
1 (14-ounce) can EAGLE BRAND® Sweetened Condensed Milk (NOT evaporated milk)
2 teaspoons grated lemon peel
¾ cup (1½ sticks) plus 2 tablespoons cold butter or margarine, divided
2 cups biscuit baking mix, divided
½ cup firmly packed light brown sugar
½ cup chopped nuts
Vanilla ice cream
Blueberry Sauce (recipe follows)

Fudge Ribbon Cake

1 (18.25-ounce) package chocolate cake mix, plus ingredients to prepare mix

1 (8-ounce) package cream cheese, softened

2 tablespoons butter or margarine, softened

1 tablespoon cornstarch

1 (14-ounce) can EAGLE BRAND® Sweetened Condensed Milk (NOT evaporated milk)

1 egg

1 teaspoon vanilla extract Chocolate Glaze (recipe follows)

1. Preheat oven to 350°F. Grease and flour 13×9-inch baking pan. Prepare cake mix as package directs. Pour batter into prepared pan.

2. In small bowl, beat cream cheese, butter and cornstarch until fluffy. Gradually beat in EAGLE BRAND®. Add egg and vanilla; beat until smooth. Spoon evenly over cake batter.

3. Bake 40 minutes or until wooden pick inserted near center comes out clean. Cool. Prepare Chocolate Glaze and drizzle over cake. Store leftovers covered in refrigerator.   *Makes 10 to 12 servings*

Chocolate Glaze: In small saucepan over low heat, melt 1 (1-ounce) square unsweetened or semisweet chocolate and 1 tablespoon butter or margarine with 2 tablespoons water. Remove from heat. Stir in ³/₄ cup powdered sugar and ¹/₂ teaspoon vanilla extract. Stir until smooth and well blended. Makes about ¹/₃ cup glaze.

Prep Time: *20 minutes*
Bake Time: *40 minutes*

Fudge Ribbon Bundt Cake: Preheat oven to 350°F. Grease and flour 10-inch Bundt pan. Prepare cake mix as package directs. Pour batter into prepared pan. Prepare cream cheese layer as directed above; spoon evenly over batter. Bake 50 to 55 minutes or until wooden pick inserted near center comes out clean. Cool 10 minutes. Remove from pan. Cool. Prepare Chocolate Glaze and drizzle over cake. Store leftovers covered in refrigerator.

Desserts

Creamy Caramel Flan

1. Preheat oven to 350°F. In heavy skillet over medium heat, cook and stir sugar until melted and caramel-colored. Carefully pour into 8 ungreased 6-ounce custard cups, tilting to coat bottoms.

2. In large bowl, beat eggs; stir in water, EAGLE BRAND®, vanilla and salt. Pour into prepared custard cups. Set cups in large shallow pan. Fill pan with 1 inch hot water.

3. Bake 25 minutes or until knife inserted near centers comes out clean. Cool. Chill. To serve, invert flans onto individual serving plates. Top with Sugar Garnish (optional), or garnish as desired. Store covered in refrigerator.

Makes 8 servings

Sugar Garnish: Fill medium metal bowl half-full of ice. In medium saucepan over medium-high heat, combine 1 cup sugar with ¼ cup water. Stir; cover and bring to a boil. Cook over high heat 5 to 6 minutes or until light brown in color. Immediately place pan in ice for 1 minute. Using spoon, carefully drizzle sugar decoratively over foil. Cool. To serve, peel sugar garnish from foil.

Prep Time: *15 minutes*
Bake Time: *25 minutes*

¾ **cup sugar**
4 **eggs**
1¾ **cups water**
1 **(14-ounce) can EAGLE BRAND® Sweetened Condensed Milk (NOT evaporated milk)**
1 **teaspoon vanilla extract**
⅛ **teaspoon salt**
Sugar Garnish (recipe follows, optional)

Chocolate Cinnamon Bread Pudding

4 cups soft white bread cubes (5 slices)
½ cup chopped nuts
3 eggs
¼ cup unsweetened cocoa
2 teaspoons vanilla extract
1 teaspoon ground cinnamon
½ teaspoon salt
2¾ cups water
1 (14-ounce) can EAGLE BRAND® Sweetened Condensed Milk (NOT evaporated milk)
2 tablespoons butter or margarine, melted
Cinnamon Cream Sauce (recipe follows)

1. Preheat oven to 350°F. Place bread cubes and nuts in buttered 9-inch square baking pan. In large bowl, beat eggs, cocoa, vanilla, cinnamon and salt. Add water, EAGLE BRAND® and butter; mix well. Pour evenly over bread, moistening completely.

2. Bake 40 to 45 minutes or until knife inserted in center comes out clean. Cool slightly. Serve warm topped with Cinnamon Cream Sauce. Store leftovers covered in refrigerator. *Makes 6 to 9 servings*

Cinnamon Cream Sauce: In medium saucepan over medium-high heat, combine 1 cup whipping cream, ⅔ cup firmly packed light brown sugar, 1 teaspoon vanilla extract and ½ teaspoon ground cinnamon. Bring to a boil; reduce heat and boil rapidly 6 to 8 minutes or until thickened, stirring occasionally. Serve warm.

Desserts

Date and Nut Roll

1. In large bowl, combine wafer crumbs, dates and nuts. In small bowl, combine EAGLE BRAND® and lemon juice. Add to crumb mixture and knead well. Form into roll (3 inches in diameter) and cover with wax paper. Chill in refrigerator 12 hours or longer.

2. Cut chilled roll into slices. Garnish with whipped cream or drizzle leftover EAGLE BRAND® over slices. *Makes 8 servings*

2 cups vanilla wafer crumbs
1 cup chopped dates
½ cup chopped nuts
½ cup EAGLE BRAND® Sweetened Condensed Milk (NOT evaporated milk)
2 teaspoons lemon juice from concentrate

Desserts

Chocolate Ice Cream Cups

2 cups (12 ounces) semisweet chocolate chips
1 (14-ounce) can EAGLE BRAND® Sweetened Condensed Milk (NOT evaporated milk)
1 cup finely ground pecans
Ice cream, any flavor

1. In heavy saucepan over low heat, melt chocolate chips with EAGLE BRAND®; remove from heat. Stir in pecans. In individual paper-lined muffin cups, spread about 2 tablespoons chocolate mixture. With lightly greased spoon, spread chocolate on bottom and up side of each cup.

2. Freeze 2 hours or until firm. Before serving, remove paper liners. Fill chocolate cups with ice cream. Store unfilled cups tightly covered in freezer.

Makes about 1½ dozen cups

Note: It is easier to remove the paper liners if the chocolate cups sit at room temperature for about 5 minutes first.

Desserts

Creamy Banana Pudding

1. In large bowl, combine EAGLE BRAND® and water. Add pudding mix; beat until well blended. Chill 5 minutes.

2. Fold in whipped cream. Spoon 1 cup pudding mixture into 2½-quart glass serving bowl or divide it among 8 to 10 individual serving dishes.

3. Top with one-third each of vanilla wafers, bananas and pudding mixture. Repeat layering twice, ending with pudding mixture. Chill. Garnish as desired. Store leftovers covered in refrigerator. *Makes 8 to 10 servings*

Prep Time: *15 minutes*

1 (14-ounce) can EAGLE BRAND® Sweetened Condensed Milk (NOT evaporated milk)
1½ cups cold water
1 (4-serving-size) package instant vanilla pudding and pie filling mix
2 cups (1 pint) whipping cream, whipped
36 vanilla wafers
3 medium bananas, sliced and dipped in lemon juice from concentrate

Desserts

Chocolate Pudding

1 (14-ounce) can EAGLE
  BRAND® Sweetened
  Condensed Milk
  (NOT evaporated milk)
2 cups water, divided
¼ teaspoon salt
3 (1-ounce) squares
  unsweetened
  chocolate
3 tablespoons cornstarch
1 teaspoon vanilla extract

1. In top of double boiler, combine EAGLE BRAND®, 1½ cups water and salt. Add chocolate. Cook over hot water; stir until chocolate melts. Gradually stir remaining ½ cup water into cornstarch, keeping mixture smooth. Gradually add to milk mixture; stir rapidly. Continue to cook, stirring constantly until thickened. Stir in vanilla.

2. Divide pudding evenly among six individual dessert dishes. Refrigerate until ready to serve. *Makes 6 (½-cup) servings*

Chocolate Mousse Cake

1 (18.25- or 18.5-ounce)
  package chocolate
  cake mix, plus
  ingredients to prepare
  mix
1 (14-ounce) can EAGLE
  BRAND® Sweetened
  Condensed Milk
  (NOT evaporated milk)
2 (1-ounce) squares
  unsweetened
  chocolate, melted
½ cup cold water
1 (4-serving-size) package
  instant chocolate
  pudding and pie filling
  mix
1 cup (½ pint) whipping
  cream, whipped

1. Preheat oven to 350°F. Prepare and bake cake mix as package directs for two 9-inch layers. Remove cakes from pans; cool.

2. In large bowl, beat EAGLE BRAND® and chocolate until well blended. Gradually beat in water and pudding mix until smooth. Chill 30 minutes. Beat until smooth. Fold in whipped cream.

3. Chill at least 1 hour. Place 1 cake layer on serving plate; top with 1½ cups mousse mixture. Top with remaining cake layer. Frost side and top of cake with remaining mousse mixture. *Makes 1 (9-inch) layer cake*

Banana Split Dessert Pizza

1. Preheat oven to 375°F. For filling, in medium bowl, combine EAGLE BRAND®, sour cream, ¼ cup lemon juice and vanilla; mix well. Chill.

2. In large bowl, beat ½ cup butter and brown sugar until fluffy. Add flour and nuts; mix well.

3. On lightly greased pizza pan or baking sheet; press dough into 12-inch circle, forming rim around edge. Prick with fork. Bake 10 to 12 minutes or until golden brown. Cool.

4. Arrange 2 sliced bananas on cooled crust. Spoon filling evenly over bananas. Dip remaining banana slices in remaining 2 tablespoons lemon juice; arrange on top along with pineapple, cherries and additional nuts.

5. In small saucepan over low heat, melt chocolate with remaining 1 tablespoon butter; drizzle over pizza. Chill thoroughly. Store leftovers covered in refrigerator.   *Makes 1 (12-inch) pizza*

1 (14-ounce) can EAGLE BRAND® Sweetened Condensed Milk (NOT evaporated milk)
½ cup sour cream
¼ cup plus 2 tablespoons lemon juice from concentrate, divided
1 teaspoon vanilla extract
½ cup (1 stick) plus 1 tablespoon butter, softened and divided
¼ cup firmly packed light brown sugar
1 cup all-purpose flour
¾ cup chopped nuts
3 medium bananas, sliced and divided
1 (8-ounce) can sliced pineapple, drained and cut in half
9 maraschino cherries drained and patted dry
Additional nuts for garnish
1 (1-ounce) square semisweet chocolate

Desserts

Rich Caramel Cake

1 (14-ounce) package
    caramels, unwrapped
½ cup (1 stick) butter or
    margarine
1 (14-ounce) can EAGLE
    BRAND® Sweetened
    Condensed Milk
    (NOT evaporated milk)
1 (18.25- or 18.5-ounce)
    package chocolate
    cake mix, plus
    ingredients to prepare
    mix
1 cup coarsely chopped
    pecans

1. Preheat oven to 350°F. In heavy saucepan over low heat, melt caramels and butter. Remove from heat; add EAGLE BRAND®. Mix well; set aside. Prepare cake mix as package directs.

2. Spread 2 cups cake batter into greased 13×9-inch baking pan; bake 15 minutes. Spread caramel mixture evenly over cake; spread remaining cake batter over caramel mixture. Top with pecans. Bake 30 to 35 minutes or until cake springs back when lightly touched. Cool.

Makes 10 to 12 servings

Desserts

Classic Vanilla Ice Cream

1. Split vanilla bean lengthwise; scrape out seeds and discard bean. In large bowl, combine all ingredients; mix well.

2. Pour into ice cream freezer container. Freeze according to manufacturer's instructions.

Makes about 1½ quarts ice cream

Delicious Homemade Milkshakes: Combine 2 large scoops of ice cream with 1 cup milk in blender; blend in flavored syrups or fruits, if desired.

Fantastic Sundaes: Top scoops of ice cream with flavored syrups, fresh fruits, crushed candies or crumbled cookies. Add a dollop of whipped cream and the ever-popular cherry.

Homemade Ice Cream Sandwiches: Place a scoop of ice cream on a homemade or packaged cookie; top with another cookie. For a festive touch, roll the sandwich edge in crushed candy, chopped nuts or toasted coconut. Wrap individually in foil and freeze.

À La Mode Desserts: Design your own signature desserts by topping brownies, waffles or pound cake slices with a scoop of ice cream and fresh fruit, syrup or nuts.

**1 vanilla bean *or*
   2 tablespoons vanilla
   extract
2 cups (1 pint) half-and-
   half
2 cups (1 pint) whipping
   cream
1 (14-ounce) can EAGLE
   BRAND® Sweetened
   Condensed Milk
   (NOT evaporated milk)**

Chocolate Cream Crêpes

1 (14-ounce) can EAGLE BRAND® Sweetened Condensed Milk (NOT evaporated milk)

¼ cup cold water

1 (4-serving-size) package instant chocolate pudding and pie filling mix

¼ cup unsweetened cocoa

1 cup (½ pint) whipping cream, whipped

1 (4½-ounce) package ready-to-use crêpes (10 crêpes)

1½ cups sliced or cut-up fresh fruit such as strawberries, peaches or raspberries

Powdered sugar

1. In large bowl, beat EAGLE BRAND® and water. Beat in pudding mix and cocoa. Fold in whipped cream. Cover and chill 15 minutes.

2. Pipe or spoon generous ⅓ cup filling into center of each crêpe. Roll up each crêpe. Place on serving plate. Spoon fruit over crêpes. Sprinkle with powdered sugar. Store leftovers covered in refrigerator.   *Makes 5 servings*

Prep Time: *10 minutes plus assembling*
Chill Time: *15 minutes*

Holiday Coffeecake

1. Preheat oven to 350°F. In large bowl, beat biscuit mix, EAGLE BRAND®, sour cream, ¼ cup butter, eggs and ½ teaspoon cinnamon until smooth. Pour batter into lightly greased 11×7-inch baking dish.

2. In small bowl, combine pecans, brown sugar, remaining 1 tablespoon butter and remaining 1 teaspoon cinnamon. Sprinkle mixture evenly over batter. Bake 40 to 45 minutes or until wooden pick inserted in center comes out clean. Cool in dish on wire rack 10 minutes.   *Makes 8 servings*

2 cups biscuit baking mix
1 (14-ounce) can EAGLE BRAND® Sweetened Condensed Milk (NOT evaporated milk)
¾ cup sour cream
¼ cup (½ stick) plus 1 tablespoon butter or margarine, melted and divided
2 eggs
1½ teaspoons ground cinnamon, divided
½ cup chopped pecans
2 tablespoons firmly packed light brown sugar

Cool and Minty Party Cake

1 (14-ounce) can EAGLE
BRAND® Sweetened
Condensed Milk
(NOT evaporated milk)
2 teaspoons peppermint
extract
8 drops green food
coloring (optional)
2 cups (1 pint) whipping
cream, whipped (do
not use non-dairy
whipped topping)
1 (18.25- or 18.5-ounce)
package white cake
mix, plus ingredients to
prepare mix
Green crème de menthe
liqueur
1 (8-ounce) container
frozen non-dairy
whipped topping,
thawed

1. Line 9-inch round cake pan with foil. In large bowl, combine EAGLE BRAND®, peppermint extract and food coloring (optional). Fold in whipped cream. Pour into prepared pan; cover. Freeze at least 6 hours or until firm.

2. Meanwhile, prepare and bake cake mix as package directs for two 9-inch round layers. Remove from pans; cool completely.

3. With fork, poke holes in cake layers, 1 inch apart, halfway through each layer. Spoon small amounts of liqueur into holes. Place one cake layer on serving plate; top with frozen EAGLE BRAND® mixture, then second cake layer. Trim frozen layer to edge of cake layers.

4. Frost quickly with whipped topping. Return to freezer for at least 6 hours before serving. Garnish as desired. Store leftovers covered in freezer.

Makes 1 (9-inch) layer cake

Crunchy Peppermint Candy Ice Cream

1. Combine all ingredients in ice cream freezer container. Freeze according to manufacturer's instructions.

2. Garnish with additional crushed peppermint candy, if desired.

Makes 1½ quarts ice cream

1¼ cups water
1 (14-ounce) can EAGLE BRAND® Sweetened Condensed Milk (NOT evaporated milk)
2 cups (1 pint) light cream
½ cup crushed peppermint candy
1 tablespoon vanilla extract

Candies & Treats

No-Bake Peanutty Chocolate Drops

½ cup (1 stick) butter or margarine
⅓ cup unsweetened cocoa
2½ cups quick-cooking oats
1 (14-ounce) can EAGLE BRAND® Sweetened Condensed Milk (NOT evaporated milk)
1 cup chopped peanuts
½ cup peanut butter

1. Line baking sheets with wax paper. In medium saucepan over medium heat, melt butter; stir in cocoa. Bring mixture to a boil.

2. Remove from heat; stir in remaining ingredients.

3. Drop by teaspoonfuls onto prepared baking sheets; chill 2 hours or until set. Store loosely covered in refrigerator.   *Makes about 5 dozen drops*

Prep Time: *10 minutes*
Chill Time: *2 hours*

Creamy Hot Chocolate

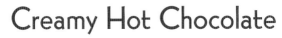

1 (14-ounce) can EAGLE
    BRAND® Sweetened
    Condensed Milk
    (NOT evaporated milk)
½ cup unsweetened cocoa
1½ teaspoons vanilla extract
⅛ teaspoon salt
6½ cups hot water
    Marshmallows (optional)

1. In large saucepan over medium heat, combine EAGLE BRAND®, cocoa, vanilla and salt; mix well.

2. Slowly stir in water. Heat through, stirring occasionally. Do not boil. Top with marshmallows (optional). Store covered in refrigerator.

Makes about 2 quarts hot chocolate

Prep Time: *8 to 10 minutes*

Microwave Directions: In 2-quart glass measure, combine all ingredients except marshmallows. Microwave at HIGH (100% power) 8 to 10 minutes, stirring every 3 minutes. Top with marshmallows (optional). Store covered in refrigerator.

Tip: Hot chocolate can be stored in the refrigerator for up to 5 days. Mix well and reheat before serving.

Serving Suggestion: For a decadent treat, serve with Festive Fudge (page 146).

Candies & Treats

Chocolate Raspberry Truffles

1. In large microwave-safe bowl, combine EAGLE BRAND®, liqueur, butter and jam. Microwave at HIGH (100% power) 3 minutes.

2. Stir in chocolate chips until smooth. Cover and chill 1 hour.

3. Shape mixture into 1-inch balls; roll in powdered sugar or almonds. Store covered at room temperature.
 Makes 4 dozen truffles

Prep Time: *10 minutes*
Cook Time: *3 minutes*
Chill Time: *1 hour*

1 (14-ounce) can EAGLE BRAND® Sweetened Condensed Milk (NOT evaporated milk)
¼ cup raspberry liqueur
2 tablespoons butter or margarine
2 tablespoons seedless raspberry jam
2 (12-ounce) packages semisweet chocolate chips
½ cup powdered sugar or ground toasted almonds

Candies & Treats

Peanut Butter Fudge

2 (10-ounce) packages peanut butter-flavored chips
1 (14-ounce) can EAGLE BRAND® Sweetened Condensed Milk (NOT evaporated milk)
¼ cup (½ stick) butter or margarine, cut into pieces
1 cup chopped salted peanuts
Additional chopped salted peanuts (optional)

1. Butter 8-inch square dish. In 2-quart microwave-safe bowl, combine peanut butter chips, EAGLE BRAND® and butter. Microwave at MEDIUM (50% power) 4 to 5 minutes, stirring at 1½-minute intervals.

2. Stir in peanuts and pour into prepared dish. Garnish with additional chopped peanuts (optional). Cover and chill 2 hours. Cut into squares. Store covered in refrigerator.
Makes 2 pounds fudge

Prep Time: *5 minutes*
Cook Time: *4 to 5 minutes*
Chill Time: *2 hours*

Candies & Treats

Strawberry Bonbons

1. In large bowl, combine EAGLE BRAND®, coconut, ⅓ cup gelatin, almonds, almond extract and enough red food coloring to tint mixture to desired strawberry red shade. Transfer mixture to food processor and pulse several times to form paste. Chill until firm enough to handle. Shape spoonfuls of coconut mixture (about ¾ tablespoon) into strawberry shapes.

2. Sprinkle remaining gelatin on flat dish; roll each strawberry in gelatin to coat. Place on wax-paper-lined baking sheet; refrigerate.

3. To make frosting "hulls," combine powdered sugar, cream and green food coloring until well blended. Fill pastry bag fitted with open star tip with frosting; pipe small amount on top of each strawberry to form hull. Store tightly covered in refrigerator.

Makes about 2½ pounds or about 4 dozen candies

1 (14-ounce) can EAGLE BRAND® Sweetened Condensed Milk (NOT evaporated milk)
4 (3½-ounce) cans flaked coconut
1 (6-ounce) package strawberry-flavored gelatin
1 cup ground blanched almonds
1 teaspoon almond extract
Red food coloring
2 cups sifted powdered sugar
½ cup whipping cream
Green food coloring

Magic Rum Balls

4 cups coarsely chopped
    vanilla wafers
1 (14-ounce) can EAGLE
    BRAND® Sweetened
    Condensed Milk
    (NOT evaporated milk)
1 cup finely chopped
    walnuts
⅓ cup rum
    Powdered sugar

1. In large bowl, combine wafers, EAGLE BRAND®, walnuts and rum; mix well. Chill 4 hours or overnight.

2. Dip palms of hands in powdered sugar; shape wafer mixture by teaspoons into 1-inch balls. Roll in powdered sugar. (If mixture becomes too soft, rechill). Cover and store in refrigerator. Reroll in powdered sugar before serving, if desired.
Makes about 5 dozen balls

Tip: The flavor of these candies improves after 24 hours. They may be made ahead and stored in the refrigerator for several weeks.

Fudgy Coconut Clusters

1 (14-ounce) package
    flaked coconut
1 (14-ounce) can EAGLE
    BRAND® Sweetened
    Condensed Milk
    (NOT evaporated milk)
⅔ cup unsweetened cocoa
¼ cup (½ stick) butter,
    melted
2 teaspoons vanilla extract
1½ teaspoons almond extract
    Semisweet chocolate
    chips or candied
    cherries, cut into slices
    (optional)

1. Preheat oven to 350°F. Line baking sheets with foil; generously grease foil with solid vegetable shortening.

2. In large bowl, combine coconut, EAGLE BRAND®, cocoa, melted butter, vanilla and almond extract; mix well. Drop by rounded spoonfuls onto prepared baking sheets.

3. Bake 9 to 11 minutes or just until set; press 3 chocolate chips or candied cherry slices in center (optional). Immediately remove cookies from foil to wire rack; cool. Store loosely covered at room temperature.
Makes about 2½ dozen cookies

Chocolate Chip Clusters: Omit melted butter and cocoa; stir together other ingredients. Add 1 cup miniature semisweet chocolate chips; proceed as directed above.

Candies & Treats

Party Mints

1. In medium bowl, beat EAGLE BRAND® and half of powdered sugar until blended. Gradually add remaining powdered sugar and peppermint extract, beating until stiff.

2. Shape mixture into ½-inch balls. Roll in desired sugar; place on parchment paper. Let stand 8 hours to set. Store covered at room temperature.

Makes 3 dozen mints

Prep Time: *30 minutes*
Stand Time: *8 hours*

Tip: For the smoothest texture, be sure to sift the powdered sugar before mixing. It will remove any lumps and make the mints extra creamy.

Variation: You may also dip uncoated mints in melted bittersweet chocolate for a different flavor.

1 (14-ounce) can EAGLE BRAND® Sweetened Condensed Milk (NOT evaporated milk)
5½ cups powdered sugar
½ teaspoon peppermint extract
Assorted colored granulated sugar or crystals

Candies & Treats

Candy Crunch

4 cups (half of 15-ounce bag) pretzel sticks or pretzel twists

1 (14-ounce) can EAGLE BRAND® Sweetened Condensed Milk (NOT evaporated milk)

2 (10- to 12-ounce) packages premium white chocolate chips

1 cup dried fruit, such as dried cranberries, raisins or mixed dried fruit bits

1. Line 15×10×1-inch baking pan with foil. Place pretzels in large bowl.

2. In large saucepan over medium-low heat, heat EAGLE BRAND® until warm, about 5 minutes. Remove from heat; immediately stir in white chocolate chips until melted. Pour over pretzels; stir to coat.

3. Immediately spread mixture in prepared pan. Sprinkle with dried fruit; press down lightly with back of spoon.

4. Chill 1 to 2 hours or until set. Break into chunks. Store loosely covered at room temperature.   *Makes about 1¾ pounds candy*

Prep Time: *15 minutes*
Chill Time: *1 to 2 hours*

Candies & Treats

Chocolate Swizzle Nog

1. In medium saucepan over medium heat, combine milk, EAGLE BRAND® and cocoa. Heat through, stirring constantly. Remove from heat; stir in vanilla or peppermint extract.

2. Serve warm in mugs topped with whipped cream. *Makes 4 servings*

Prep Time: *5 minutes*

2 cups milk
1 (14-ounce) can EAGLE BRAND® Sweetened Condensed Milk (NOT evaporated milk)
2 tablespoons unsweetened cocoa
½ teaspoon vanilla or peppermint extract
Whipped cream or whipped topping

Golden Snacking Granola

2 cups oats
1½ cups slivered almonds or
    coarsely chopped
    walnuts
1 (3½-ounce) can flaked
    coconut (1⅓ cups)
½ cup sunflower seeds
½ cup wheat germ
2 tablespoons sesame seeds
1 teaspoon ground
    cinnamon
1 teaspoon salt
1 (14-ounce) can EAGLE
    BRAND® Sweetened
    Condensed Milk
    (NOT evaporated milk)
¼ cup vegetable oil
1 cup banana chips
    (optional)
1 cup raisins

1. Preheat oven to 300°F.

2. In large bowl, combine all ingredients except banana chips and raisins; mix well.

3. Spread evenly in foil-lined 15×10×1-inch baking pan or baking sheet.

4. Bake 55 to 60 minutes, stirring every 15 minutes. Remove from oven; stir in banana chips (optional) and raisins.

5. Cool completely. Store tightly covered at room temperature.

Makes about 2½ quarts granola

Prep Time: *15 minutes*
Bake Time: *55 to 60 minutes*

Vanilla Caramels

1 cup sugar
1 (14-ounce) can EAGLE
    BRAND® Sweetened
    Condensed Milk
    (NOT evaporated milk)
Dash salt
1 tablespoon butter or
    margarine
½ teaspoon vanilla extract

1. Butter 8-inch square baking dish; set aside. Place sugar in heavy saucepan over low heat and stir constantly to prevent burning; stir until melted and the color of maple syrup. Gradually add EAGLE BRAND® and salt. Cook over low heat about 15 minutes (do not overcook). Remove from heat; add butter and vanilla. Immediately pour into prepared dish. Cool completely.

2. When caramel is completely cooled, remove from pan and cut into squares.

Makes 1¼ pounds caramels

Strawberry Splash Punch

1. In blender container, combine 1½ cups strawberries and lemon juice; cover and blend until smooth.

2. Add EAGLE BRAND®; cover and blend. Pour into large pitcher. Gradually stir in carbonated beverage. Add ice (optional). Garnish each serving with whole strawberry (optional). *Makes 10 servings*

Prep Time: *10 minutes*

1½ cups fresh whole strawberries

½ cup lemon juice from concentrate, chilled

1 (14-ounce) can EAGLE BRAND® Sweetened Condensed Milk (NOT evaporated milk), chilled

1 (1-liter) bottle strawberry-flavored carbonated beverage, chilled

Ice cubes (optional)

Fresh whole strawberries (optional)

Candies & Treats

Chilled Café Latte

2 tablespoons instant
    coffee
¾ cup warm water
1 (14-ounce) can EAGLE
    BRAND® Sweetened
    Condensed Milk
    (NOT evaporated milk)
1 teaspoon vanilla extract
4 cups ice cubes

1. Dissolve coffee in water in blender container. Add EAGLE BRAND® and vanilla; blend on high speed until well mixed.

2. Gradually add ice to blender, blending until smooth. Serve immediately. Store leftovers covered in refrigerator.

Makes 4 servings or about 5 cups latte

Candies & Treats

Layered Mint Chocolate Fudge

1. Line 8- or 9-inch square pan with wax paper. In heavy saucepan over low heat, melt semisweet chocolate chips with 1 cup EAGLE BRAND®. Stir in vanilla. Spread half the mixture in prepared pan; chill 10 minutes or until firm. Keep remaining chocolate mixture at room temperature.

2. In heavy saucepan over low heat, melt white chocolate chips with remaining EAGLE BRAND®. Stir in peppermint extract and food coloring (optional). Spread over chilled chocolate layer; chill 10 minutes or until firm. Spread reserved chocolate mixture over mint layer. Chill 2 hours or until firm.

3. Turn fudge onto cutting board; peel off paper and cut into squares. Store loosely covered at room temperature.   *Makes about 1¾ pounds fudge*

Prep Time: *20 minutes*
Chill Time: *2 hours 20 minutes*

1 (12-ounce) package semisweet chocolate chips
1 (14-ounce) can EAGLE BRAND® Sweetened Condensed Milk (NOT evaporated milk), divided
2 teaspoons vanilla extract
1 cup (6 ounces) premium white chocolate chips *or* 6 ounces vanilla-flavored candy coating*
1 tablespoon peppermint extract
2 to 3 drops green or red food coloring (optional)

*Also called confectionery coating or almond bark. If it is not available in your local supermarket, it can be purchased in candy specialty stores.

Candies & Treats

Peppermint Chocolate Fudge

2 cups (12 ounces) milk chocolate chips
1 cup (6 ounces) semisweet chocolate chips
1 (14-ounce) can EAGLE BRAND® Sweetened Condensed Milk (NOT evaporated milk)
Dash salt
½ teaspoon peppermint extract
¼ cup crushed hard peppermint candy

1. In heavy saucepan over low heat, melt milk and semisweet chocolate chips with EAGLE BRAND® and salt. Remove from heat; stir in peppermint extract. Spread evenly in wax-paper-lined 8- or 9-inch square pan. Sprinkle with peppermint candy.

2. Chill 2 hours or until firm. Turn fudge onto cutting board; peel off paper and cut into squares. Store covered in refrigerator.

Makes about 2 pounds fudge

Prep Time: *10 minutes*
Chill Time: *2 hours*

White Truffles

1. In heavy saucepan over low heat, melt vanilla candy coating with EAGLE BRAND®. Remove from heat; stir in vanilla. Cool.

2. Shape into 1-inch balls. With wooden pick, partially dip each ball into melted chocolate candy coating or roll in cocoa. Place on wax-paper-lined baking sheets until firm. Store covered at room temperature or in refrigerator.

Makes about 8 dozen truffles

Flavoring Options: **Amaretto:** Omit vanilla. Add 3 tablespoons amaretto or other almond-flavored liqueur and ½ teaspoon almond extract. Roll in finely chopped toasted almonds. **Orange:** Omit vanilla. Add 3 tablespoons orange-flavored liqueur. Roll in finely chopped toasted almonds mixed with finely grated orange peel. **Rum:** Omit vanilla. Add ¼ cup dark rum. Roll in flaked coconut. **Bourbon:** Omit vanilla. Add 3 tablespoons bourbon. Roll in finely chopped toasted nuts.

2 pounds vanilla-flavored candy coating*
1 (14-ounce) can EAGLE BRAND® Sweetened Condensed Milk (NOT evaporated milk)
1 tablespoon vanilla extract
1 pound chocolate-flavored candy coating,* melted, or unsweetened cocoa

*Also called confectionery coating or almond bark. If it is not available in your local supermarket, it can be purchased in candy specialty stores.

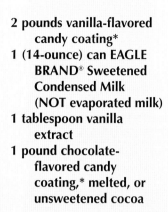

Homemade Cream Liqueur

1 (14-ounce) can EAGLE
    BRAND® Sweetened
    Condensed Milk
    (NOT evaporated milk)
1¼ cups flavored liqueur
    (almond, coffee,
    orange or mint)
2 cups (1 pint) whipping
    cream or coffee cream

1. In blender container, combine all ingredients; blend until smooth.

2. To serve, pour into glasses over ice. Garnish as desired. Store tightly covered in refrigerator. Stir before serving.   *Makes about 1 quart liqueur*

Prep Time: *5 minutes*

Dulce de Leche

1 (14-ounce) can EAGLE
    BRAND® Sweetened
    Condensed Milk
    (NOT evaporated milk)
Assorted dippers, such as
    cookies, pound cake
    cubes, angel food cake
    cubes, banana chunks,
    orange slices, apple
    slices and/or
    strawberries

1. Preheat oven to 425°F. Pour EAGLE BRAND® into ungreased 9-inch pie plate. Cover with foil; place in larger shallow baking pan. Pour hot water into larger pan to depth of 1 inch.

2. Bake 1 hour or until thick and caramel-colored. Beat until smooth. Cool 1 hour. Refrigerate until serving time. Serve as dip with assorted dippers. Store covered in refrigerator for up to 1 week.   *Makes about 1¼ cups dip*

Prep Time: *5 minutes*
Bake Time: *1 hour*
Cool Time: *1 hour*

CAUTION: Never heat an unopened can.

Hot Fudge Sauce

1. In heavy saucepan over medium heat, melt chocolate chips and butter with EAGLE BRAND® and water. Cook and stir constantly until smooth. Stir in vanilla.

2. Serve warm over ice cream or as dipping sauce for fruit. Store leftovers covered in refrigerator.

Makes 2 cups sauce

Prep Time: *10 minutes*

Microwave Directions: In 1-quart glass measure, combine all ingredients. Microwave at HIGH (100% power) 3 to 3½ minutes, stirring after each minute.

To Reheat: In small heavy saucepan, combine desired amount of Hot Fudge Sauce with small amount of water. Over low heat, stir constantly until heated through.

Spirited Hot Fudge Sauce: Add ¼ cup almond, coffee, mint or orange-flavored liqueur with vanilla.

Serving Suggestion: For a wonderful dessert duo, serve with Dulce de Leche (page 138).

1 cup (6 ounces) semisweet chocolate chips *or*
4 (1-ounce) squares semisweet chocolate
2 tablespoons butter or margarine
1 (14-ounce) can EAGLE BRAND® Sweetened Condensed Milk (NOT evaporated milk)
2 tablespoons water
1 teaspoon vanilla extract

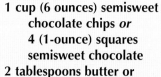

S'Mores on a Stick

1 (14-ounce) can EAGLE
    BRAND® Sweetened
    Condensed Milk
    (NOT evaporated
    milk), divided
1½ cups milk chocolate
    chips, divided
1 cup miniature
    marshmallows
11 whole graham crackers,
    halved crosswise
Toppings: chopped
    peanuts, miniature
    candy-coated
    chocolate pieces,
    sprinkles

1. In microwave-safe bowl, microwave half of EAGLE BRAND® at HIGH (100% power) 1½ minutes. Stir in 1 cup chocolate chips until smooth; stir in marshmallows.

2. Spread chocolate mixture evenly by heaping tablespoonfuls onto 11 graham cracker halves. Top with remaining graham cracker halves; place on wax paper.

3. Microwave remaining EAGLE BRAND® at HIGH (100% power) 1½ minutes; stir in remaining ½ cup chocolate chips, stirring until smooth. Drizzle mixture over treats; sprinkle with desired toppings.

4. Let stand for 2 hours; insert wooden craft stick into center of each treat.

Makes 11 servings

Prep Time: *10 minutes*
Cook Time: *3 minutes*

Candies & Treats

Banana Smoothies & Pops

1. In blender container, combine all ingredients; blend until smooth, scraping down sides occasionally.

2. Serve immediately. Store leftovers covered in refrigerator.

Makes 4 (1-cup) servings

Prep Time: *5 minutes*

Banana Smoothie Pops: Spoon banana mixture into 8 (5-ounce) paper cups. Freeze 30 minutes. Insert wooden craft sticks into center of each cup; freeze until firm. Makes 8 pops.

Fruit Smoothies: Substitute 1 cup of your favorite fruit and ½ cup any fruit juice for banana and orange juice.

1 (14-ounce) can EAGLE BRAND® Sweetened Condensed Milk (NOT evaporated milk)
1 (8-ounce) container vanilla yogurt
2 ripe bananas
½ cup orange juice

Candies & Treats

Dipsy Doodles Butterscotch Dip

1 (14-ounce) can EAGLE BRAND® Sweetened Condensed Milk (NOT evaporated milk)

1½ cups milk

1 (4-serving-size) package cook-and-serve butterscotch pudding and pie filling mix

Apples or pears, cored and sliced, or banana chunks

1. In medium saucepan over medium heat, combine EAGLE BRAND®, milk and pudding mix. Cook and stir until thickened and bubbly; cook 2 minutes more.

2. Cool slightly. Pour into serving bowl or individual cups. Serve warm with fruit.

Makes about 2½ cups dip

Prep Time: *15 minutes*

Tip: Store leftovers covered in the refrigerator. Reheat and serve as a sauce over vanilla ice cream. Sprinkle sauce with miniature semisweet chocolate chips or toasted nuts, if desired.

Candies & Treats

Chocolate Snow Swirl Fudge

1. Line 8-inch square pan with foil, extending foil over edges of pan. Butter foil; set aside. In saucepan over low heat, melt chocolate chips with EAGLE BRAND®, 2 tablespoons butter and salt. Remove from heat; stir in vanilla and nuts. Spread evenly in prepared pan.

2. In small saucepan over low heat, melt marshmallows with remaining 2 tablespoons butter; stir until smooth. Spread on top of fudge. With table knife or metal spatula, swirl through top of fudge.

3. Chill at least 2 hours or until firm. Turn fudge out onto cutting board; peel off foil and cut into squares. Store covered in refrigerator.

Makes about 2 pounds fudge

3 cups semisweet chocolate chips
1 (14-ounce) can EAGLE BRAND® Sweetened Condensed Milk (NOT evaporated milk)
¼ cup (½ stick) butter or margarine, divided
Dash salt
1½ teaspoons vanilla extract
1 cup chopped nuts
2 cups miniature marshmallows

Candies & Treats

White Christmas Jewel Fudge

3 cups premium white chocolate chips

1 (14-ounce) can EAGLE BRAND® Sweetened Condensed Milk (NOT evaporated milk)

1½ teaspoons vanilla extract

⅛ teaspoon salt

½ cup chopped green candied cherries

½ cup chopped red candied cherries

1. In heavy saucepan over low heat, melt white chocolate chips with EAGLE BRAND®, vanilla and salt. Remove from heat; stir in cherries. Spread evenly into wax-paper-lined 8- or 9-inch square pan. Chill 2 hours or until firm.

2. Turn fudge onto cutting board; peel off paper and cut into squares. Store covered in refrigerator.   *Makes 2¼ pounds fudge*

Tip: Fudge makes a great homemade holiday gift!

Candies & Treats

Homemade Irish Cream Liqueur

1. In blender container, combine all ingredients; blend until smooth. Serve over ice.

2. Store tightly covered in refrigerator. Stir before serving.

Makes about 5 cups liqueur

Tip: For a more blended flavor, store the liqueur in the refrigerator for several hours before serving.

2 cups whipping cream or coffee cream
1 (14-ounce) can EAGLE BRAND® Sweetened Condensed Milk (NOT evaporated milk)
1¼ to 1¾ cups Irish whiskey, brandy, rum, bourbon, Scotch or rye whiskey
2 tablespoons chocolate-flavored syrup
2 teaspoons instant coffee
1 teaspoon vanilla extract
½ teaspoon almond extract

Candies & Treats

Festive Fudge

3 cups semisweet or milk chocolate chips
1 (14-ounce) can EAGLE BRAND® Sweetened Condensed Milk (NOT evaporated milk)
Dash salt
½ to 1 cup chopped nuts (optional)
1½ teaspoons vanilla extract

1. Line 8- or 9-inch square pan with foil, extending foil over edges of pan. Butter foil; set aside. In heavy saucepan over low heat, melt chocolate chips with EAGLE BRAND® and salt. Remove from heat; stir in nuts (optional) and vanilla. Spread evenly in prepared pan.

2. Chill 2 hours or until firm. Turn fudge onto cutting board; peel off foil and cut into squares. Store covered in refrigerator.

Makes about 2 pounds fudge

Chocolate Peanut Butter Chip Glazed Fudge: Substitute ¾ cup peanut butter chips for nuts. For glaze, melt additional ½ cup peanut butter chips with ½ cup whipping cream; stir until thick and smooth. Spread over fudge.

Marshmallow Fudge: Add 2 tablespoons butter to chocolate mixture. Substitute 2 cups miniature marshmallows for nuts.

Tip: Create delicious homemade gifts from an assortment of flavored fudges, packed in decorative tins, candy bags or boxes. Wrap individual pieces of fudge in colored food-grade cellophane, candy wrappers or gold or silver foil candy cups and arrange in gift bags or tins. Store in refrigerator.

Candies & Treats

Creamy Cinnamon Rolls

1. On lightly floured surface, roll each bread dough loaf into 12×9-inch rectangle. Spread ⅓ cup EAGLE BRAND® over dough rectangles. Sprinkle rectangles with 1 cup pecans and cinnamon. Roll up jelly-roll style starting from short side. Cut each log into 6 slices.

2. Generously grease 13×9-inch baking pan. Place rolls cut sides down in pan. Cover loosely with greased wax paper and then with plastic wrap. Chill overnight. Cover and chill remaining EAGLE BRAND®.

3. To bake, let pan of rolls stand at room temperature 30 minutes. Preheat oven to 350°F. Bake 30 to 35 minutes or until golden brown. Cool in pan 5 minutes; loosen edges and remove rolls from pan.

4. Meanwhile for frosting, in small bowl, combine powdered sugar, remaining ⅓ cup EAGLE BRAND® and vanilla. Drizzle frosting over warm rolls. Sprinkle with additional chopped pecans (optional).   *Makes 12 rolls*

Prep Time: *20 minutes*
Chill Time: *Overnight*
Bake Time: *30 to 35 minutes*
Cool Time: *5 minutes*

2 (1-pound) loaves frozen bread dough, thawed
⅔ cup (half of 14-ounce can*) EAGLE BRAND® Sweetened Condensed Milk (NOT evaporated milk), divided
1 cup chopped pecans
2 teaspoons ground cinnamon
1 cup sifted powdered sugar
½ teaspoon vanilla extract
Additional chopped pecans (optional)

*Use remaining EAGLE BRAND® as a dip for fruit. Pour into storage container and store tightly covered in refrigerator for up to 1 week.

Candies & Treats

Mexican Coffee

6 cups hot brewed coffee
1 (14-ounce) can EAGLE
   BRAND® Sweetened
   Condensed Milk
   (NOT evaporated milk)
½ cup coffee liqueur
2 teaspoons vanilla extract
⅓ cup tequila (optional)
   Ground cinnamon
   (optional)

1. In medium saucepan over medium heat, combine coffee, EAGLE BRAND® and liqueur. Heat through, stirring constantly. Remove from heat; stir in vanilla and tequila (optional).

2. Sprinkle each serving with cinnamon (optional). Store leftovers covered in refrigerator.   *Makes 8 cups coffee*

Make Ahead S'Mores

8 (1-ounce) squares
   semisweet chocolate
1 (14-ounce) can EAGLE
   BRAND® Sweetened
   Condensed Milk
   (NOT evaporated milk)
1 teaspoon vanilla extract
32 (4¾×2⅛-inch) whole
   graham crackers
2 cups miniature
   marshmallows

1. In heavy saucepan over low heat, melt chocolate with EAGLE BRAND® and vanilla; cook and stir until smooth.

2. Making 1 sandwich at a time, spread 1 tablespoon chocolate mixture on each of 2 whole graham crackers; sprinkle 1 graham cracker with marshmallows and gently press second graham cracker, chocolate side down, on top. Repeat with remaining ingredients.

3. Carefully break each sandwich in half before serving. Wrap with plastic wrap; store at room temperature.   *Makes 32 servings*

Peanut Butter Blocks

1. In heavy saucepan, combine EAGLE BRAND®, peanut butter, water, vanilla and salt; stir in cornstarch. Over medium heat, cook and stir until thickened and smooth.

2. Add candy coating; cook and stir until melted and smooth. Spread evenly in wax-paper-lined 9-inch square baking pan. Chill 2 hours or until firm. Cut into squares; roll firmly in peanuts to coat. Store covered at room temperature or in refrigerator. *Makes about 3 pounds candy*

Prep Time: *15 minutes*
Chill Time: *2 hours*

Microwave Method: In 1-quart glass measure, combine Eagle Brand, peanut butter, water, vanilla and salt; stir in cornstarch. Microwave at HIGH (100% power) 2 minutes; mix well. In 2-quart glass measure, melt candy coating at MEDIUM (50% power) 3 to 5 minutes, stirring after each minute. Add peanut butter mixture; mix well. Proceed as directed above.

1 (14-ounce) can EAGLE BRAND® Sweetened Condensed Milk (NOT evaporated milk)
1¼ cups creamy peanut butter
⅓ cup water
1 tablespoon vanilla extract
½ teaspoon salt
1 cup cornstarch, sifted
1 pound vanilla-flavored candy coating*
2 cups peanuts, finely chopped

*Also called confectionery coating or almond bark. If it is not available in your local supermarket, it can be purchased in candy specialty stores.

Candies & Treats

Festive Cranberry Cream Punch

Cranberry Ice Ring
  (recipe follows) or ice
1 (14-ounce) can EAGLE
  BRAND® Sweetened
  Condensed Milk
  (NOT evaporated milk)
1 (12-ounce) can frozen
  cranberry juice
  cocktail concentrate,
  thawed
1 cup cranberry-flavored
  liqueur (optional)
  Red food coloring
  (optional)
2 (1-liter) bottles club soda
  or ginger ale, chilled

1. Prepare Cranberry Ice Ring one day in advance.

2. In punch bowl, combine EAGLE BRAND®, concentrate, liqueur (optional) and food coloring (optional).

3. Just before serving, add club soda and Cranberry Ice Ring or ice. Store tightly covered in refrigerator.   *Makes about 3 quarts punch*

Cranberry Ice Ring

  2 cups cranberry juice cocktail
1½ cups water
 ¾ to 1 cup cranberries and lime slices or mint leaves

1. Combine cranberry juice cocktail and water. In 1½-quart ring mold, pour ½ cup cranberry liquid.

2. Arrange cranberries and lime slices or mint leaves in mold; freeze.

3. Add remaining 3 cups cranberry liquid to mold; freeze overnight.
          Makes 1 ice ring

Candies & Treats

Chocolate Truffles

1. In heavy saucepan over low heat, melt chocolate chips with EAGLE BRAND®. Remove from heat; stir in vanilla.

2. Chill 2 hours or until firm. Shape into 1-inch balls; roll in desired coating.

3. Chill 1 hour or until firm. Store covered at room temperature.

Makes about 6 dozen truffles

Prep Time: *10 minutes*
Chill Time: *3 hours*

Microwave Directions: In 1-quart glass measure, combine chocolate chips and EAGLE BRAND®. Microwave at HIGH (100% power) 3 minutes, stirring after 1½ minutes. Stir until smooth. Proceed as directed above.

Amaretto Truffles: Substitute 3 tablespoons amaretto liqueur and ½ teaspoon almond extract for vanilla. Roll in finely chopped toasted almonds.

Orange Truffles: Substitute 3 tablespoons orange-flavored liqueur for vanilla. Roll in finely chopped toasted almonds mixed with finely grated orange peel.

Rum Truffles: Substitute ¼ cup dark rum for vanilla. Roll in flaked coconut.

Bourbon Truffles: Substitute 3 tablespoons bourbon for vanilla. Roll in finely chopped toasted nuts.

3 cups semisweet chocolate chips
1 (14-ounce) can EAGLE BRAND® Sweetened Condensed Milk (NOT evaporated milk)
1 tablespoon vanilla extract
   Coatings: finely chopped toasted nuts, flaked coconut, chocolate sprinkles, colored sugar, unsweetened cocoa, powdered sugar or colored sprinkles

Cookies 'n' Crème Fudge

3 (6-ounce) packages white chocolate baking squares

1 (14-ounce) can EAGLE BRAND® Sweetened Condensed Milk (NOT evaporated milk)

⅛ teaspoon salt

2 cups coarsely crushed chocolate creme-filled sandwich cookies (about 20 cookies)

1. Line 8-inch square baking pan with wax paper. In heavy saucepan over low heat, melt white chocolate with EAGLE BRAND® and salt. Remove from heat. Stir in crushed cookies. Spread evenly in prepared pan.

2. Chill 2 hours or until firm. Turn fudge onto cutting board; peel off paper and cut into squares. Store tightly covered at room temperature.

Makes about 2½ pounds fudge

Prep Time: 10 minutes
Chill Time: 2 hours

Fruit Smoothies

1. In blender container, combine chilled EAGLE BRAND®, yogurt, banana, whole strawberries, pineapple with its juice and lemon juice; cover and blend until smooth.

2. With blender running, gradually add ice cubes, blending until smooth. Garnish with strawberries (optional). Serve immediately.

Makes 5 servings

Prep Time: *5 minutes*

Peach Smoothies: Omit strawberries and pineapple. Add 2 cups frozen or fresh sliced peaches. Proceed as directed above.

Key Lime Smoothies: Omit strawberries, pineapple and lemon juice. Add ⅓ cup key lime juice from concentrate. Proceed as directed above. Tint with green food coloring, if desired. Garnish with lime slices, if desired.

1 (14-ounce) can EAGLE BRAND® Sweetened Condensed Milk (NOT evaporated milk), chilled
1 (8-ounce) carton plain yogurt
1 small banana, cut up
1 cup frozen or fresh whole strawberries
1 (8-ounce) can crushed pineapple packed in juice, chilled
2 tablespoons lemon juice from concentrate
1 cup ice cubes
Additional fresh strawberries (optional)

Candies & Treats

Rocky Road Candy

1 (12-ounce) package semisweet chocolate chips

2 tablespoons butter or margarine

1 (14-ounce) can EAGLE BRAND® Sweetened Condensed Milk (NOT evaporated milk)

2 cups dry roasted peanuts

1 (10½-ounce) package miniature marshmallows

1. Line 13×9-inch baking pan with wax paper. In heavy saucepan over low heat, melt chocolate chips and butter with EAGLE BRAND®; remove from heat.

2. In large bowl, combine peanuts and marshmallows; stir in chocolate mixture. Spread in prepared pan. Chill 2 hours or until firm.

3. Remove candy from pan; peel off paper and cut into squares. Store loosely covered at room temperature.   *Makes about 3½ dozen candies*

Prep Time: *10 minutes*
Chill Time: *2 hours*

Microwave Directions: In 1-quart glass measure, combine chocolate chips, butter and EAGLE BRAND®. Microwave at HIGH (100% power) 3 minutes, stirring after 1½ minutes. Stir until chocolate chips are melted and smooth. Let stand 5 minutes. Proceed as directed above.

Index

Index

Index

Metric Conversion Chart

VOLUME MEASUREMENTS (dry)

¹/₈ teaspoon = 0.5 mL
¹/₄ teaspoon = 1 mL
¹/₂ teaspoon = 2 mL
³/₄ teaspoon = 4 mL
1 teaspoon = 5 mL
1 tablespoon = 15 mL
2 tablespoons = 30 mL
¹/₄ cup = 60 mL
¹/₃ cup = 75 mL
¹/₂ cup = 125 mL
²/₃ cup = 150 mL
³/₄ cup = 175 mL
1 cup = 250 mL
2 cups = 1 pint = 500 mL
3 cups = 750 mL
4 cups = 1 quart = 1 L

VOLUME MEASUREMENTS (fluid)

1 fluid ounce (2 tablespoons) = 30 mL
4 fluid ounces (¹/₂ cup) = 125 mL
8 fluid ounces (1 cup) = 250 mL
12 fluid ounces (1¹/₂ cups) = 375 mL
16 fluid ounces (2 cups) = 500 mL

WEIGHTS (mass)

¹/₂ ounce = 15 g
1 ounce = 30 g
3 ounces = 90 g
4 ounces = 120 g
8 ounces = 225 g
10 ounces = 285 g
12 ounces = 360 g
16 ounces = 1 pound = 450 g

DIMENSIONS

¹/₁₆ inch = 2 mm
¹/₈ inch = 3 mm
¹/₄ inch = 6 mm
¹/₂ inch = 1.5 cm
³/₄ inch = 2 cm
1 inch = 2.5 cm

OVEN TEMPERATURES

250°F = 120°C
275°F = 140°C
300°F = 150°C
325°F = 160°C
350°F = 180°C
375°F = 190°C
400°F = 200°C
425°F = 220°C
450°F = 230°C

BAKING PAN SIZES

Utensil	Size in Inches/Quarts	Metric Volume	Size in Centimeters
Baking or Cake Pan (square or rectangular)	8×8×2	2 L	20×20×5
	9×9×2	2.5 L	23×23×5
	12×8×2	3 L	30×20×5
	13×9×2	3.5 L	33×23×5
Loaf Pan	8×4×3	1.5 L	20×10×7
	9×5×3	2 L	23×13×7
Round Layer Cake Pan	8×1½	1.2 L	20×4
	9×1½	1.5 L	23×4
Pie Plate	8×1¼	750 mL	20×3
	9×1¼	1 L	23×3
Baking Dish or Casserole	1 quart	1 L	—
	1½ quart	1.5 L	—
	2 quart	2 L	—